PARTNERING WITH SPIRIT

DAVID SPANGLER

LORIAN PRESS

PARTNERING WITH SPIRIT

Copyright © 2024 David Spangler

David Spangler has asserted his right to be identified as the author of this work. All rights are reserved, including the right to reproduce this book, or portions thereof, in any form. Reviewers may quote brief passages. Artificial Intelligence (AI) use of this material is strictly prohibited.

Edited by Susan Sherman
Interior Illustrations by David Spangler
Cover Design by Asha Hossain Design LLC

Published by Lorian Press LLC
Coloma, Michigan

ISBN: 978-1-939790-64-4

Spangler/David
Partnering with Spirit/David Spangler

First Print Edition: November 2024

Printed in the United States of America
and other countries

www.lorian.org

DEDICATION

I gratefully dedicate this book to all those who are working for peace, harmony and the wholeness of our world. Blessing on their efforts.

ACKNOWLEDGMENTS

I want to acknowledge all the people who participated in my Alliance Paradigm classes through the years. Your encouragement, questions, and contributions helped me give form and coherence to this material. I owe you all a deep debt of gratitude.

I particularly want to acknowledge my Lorian colleague and friend, Jeremy Berg, whose insights about our "natural alliances" were a great help conceptually. It transformed Lorian's Alliance class and led to my writing this book.

I also wish to acknowledge the help and contribution over the years of my subtle allies and colleagues, without whose partnership none of this material would ever have seen the light of day. In a way, this book is a manifestation of their love.

Finally, I want to thank Julia, my lovely wife and partner, without whose help, inspiration, support, wisdom, and joy none of my work would be possible. In important ways, this is as much her book as mine. Thank you, Sweetheart!

CONTENTS

INTRODUCTION	1
PART I: FOUNDATIONS	2
Earth Star	3
The Subtle Ecology	4
Gaia	6
The Two Ecologies	11
An Energy Metabolism	19
Three Stages	20
PART II: THE BLESSING PARTNERSHIP	22
Self-Light	25
Self-Light Exercise 1	25
Self-Light Exercise 2	26
Touch of Love	27
Touch of Love Exercise	28
Grail Space	29
Grail Space Exercise	30
PART III: OUR NATURAL ALLIANCES	34
Presence	36
Presence Exercise	37
The Entelechy	43
Attuning to the Entelechy	44
Individuation: The Body Intelligence	45
Nature: The Incarnational Elemental	49
Humanity: The Pit Crew	53

Attuning to Your Pit Crew	61
Transincarnational: Guardian Angel	63
The Soul	65
The Challenge	70
The Response	72

PART IV: FOUNDATIONAL THOUGHTS 74

Perception: Beyond Seeing and Hearing	75
Modes of Perception	78
Perception as Participation	82
More Than Psychology	83
Imagination and Anthropomorphizing	87
Saying No!	92
It's the Incarnation	93

PART V: THE GAIAN HUMAN 96

The Stellar Earth	97
The Call of Light	101
The Human Energy System	103
RIPE	110
Touch of Love Exercise	114
The Entelechy	116
The Gaian Human	119
The Gift	129
Identity	136
The Path	138
Path of Connection Exercise	142

PART VI: THE GAIAN ALLIANCE 148

- Three Zones 149
- Modes of Connection 153
- Eco-Contact 156
- Collaborative Mind 159
- Alliance Space 160
- The Path of Contact 163
- The Personal Subtle Environment 165
- Techno-Elementals 175
- Attuning to Techno-Elemental Partners 177
- Nature Spirits and the Subtle Commons 180
- Attuning to Nature Spirit Partners 187
- Devas and Angels 188
- Devas 189
- Attuning to Devic Partners 193
- Angels 194
- Attuning to Angelic Partners 199
- The Commonwealth of Light 200
- The Path of Contact Practice 207
- Faerie 208
- The Sidhe 210
- Gaia 217
- The Path of Light 218
- Presence, Not Information 221
- Soul on the Ground 222
- The Gaian Alliance 224

Reading References 227
Partnering with Spirit Card Deck 228

INTRODUCTION

I've had contact with the non-physical or subtle worlds and with non-physical beings all my life. This gives me a body of experience on which to draw to write a book about partnering with realms of life beyond the physical. However, this needs to be seen in perspective. I could be a naturalist who has spent his life studying the flora and fauna around the Seattle area where I live, but in the process, I would know nothing about the jungles of the Amazon, the deserts of Saharan Africa, the tundra of northern Canada, or the vast prairies in the middle of the North American continent. My knowledge of the ecologies of the world would be limited. However, I would understand the principles of biology and ecology gained from the knowledge I did have, as these are universal.

The subtle worlds are vast, vaster than the physical world around us, and infinitely stranger and more varied. My experiences only touch on a tiny part of them. It's quite possible that your experiences may be different, just as a person living in the Northeast of the United States will experience a different climate from someone living in the Southwest. But both will experience *weather*, and there will be similarities between the climates. Rain in Arizona, after all, is the same as rain in Vermont.

This book is part of a series of books I've written about the subtle worlds and our interaction with them. Earlier books in this series are *Subtle Worlds: An Explorer's Field Notes*; *Working with Subtle Energies*; and *Techno-Elementals*. Other books with relevant content are *Journey into Fire* and *Partnering with Earth*. Although this book stands on its own, the previous works provide a useful context and background for what I have to say here.

PART I: FOUNDATIONS

Earth Star

Some years ago, I was conducting a workshop at a spiritual conference center in California in the beautiful rolling hill country north of the Golden Gate Bridge. This center was surrounded by hiking trails that meandered through the woods and up and down the hills. During a lunch break, I decided to take a walk along one of these trails to get some exercise and to enjoy the beauty of the place.

As I hiked along by myself, I came out of a small grove of woods and could see the trail stretching straight before me for thirty yards or so before it disappeared around the side of a hill, heading back in the direction of the center. I only took a few steps along this straight path when I felt a gathering of subtle energies around me as if I had stepped across an invisible threshold. I stopped, and as I did so, about twenty feet in front of me, a glowing green sun rose up out of the earth and hovered in the air in front of me. Although sun-like in its appearance, it was not too bright to look at. Instead, it seemed to be radiating vitality and love rather than light and heat.

As I stood there watching this vision, I heard a voice very clearly in my mind. It said, "The Earth is a star of life." Then, the green sun sank back into the earth and disappeared.

This image of our world as a vibrant green star of life, radiating vital, living energies out into the cosmos, has stayed with me ever since. It is an important image in my own understanding of Gaia, our living planet. It says that each and every living thing on Earth, from the tiniest microbe to the largest whale or the tallest tree, is the means by which this vibration of creative life is generated and shines into the universe. We are each of us a star of life, replicating in the microcosm what the Earth is in the macrocosm of the cosmos.

When we partner with other life—whether that life is

another human being, a plant, an animal, or a subtle or spiritual being of some nature—we are like stars in a galaxy, coming together and sharing our unique Light with the Light of others to create a larger whole. In each of us, a potential universe, a greater wholeness, is seeking to be born through partnership.

In partnering with spirit, that potential wholeness is always there, seeking to emerge.

The Subtle Ecology

Here is another story, one that also begins with hiking. In this case, I was following a trail in woods not far from where I live that led to the foot of a magnificent waterfall, Snoqualmie Falls, a site long held sacred by the native Snoqualmie people who originally inhabited this part of the Puget Sound area. The trail was a narrow one, winding between trees and thick undergrowth. At one point, I suddenly felt a strong tug on my shoulder, and I thought my jacket had become snagged on one of the bushes that lined the trail. Looking back, though, I realized this was not the case. The jacket hung free, and the bush seemed undisturbed. However, in that moment of stopping and looking, I realized that the "tug" had come from the subtle environment around me, something that had happened to me before when a non-physical being wished to get my attention.

Realizing this, I found myself aware of a host of nature spirits around me in the forest, busy amongst the bushes and trees doing their work. Before I could do anything other than register this, I felt my consciousness merging with a presence that seemed to be both part of the bush next to me and part of a nature spirit associated with this bush, as if it had something it wished to show me.

From this perspective, I looked around. The entire forest had transformed. I could still see the trees and bushes and undergrowth, but they were all connected with fine filaments—thousands of them—along which pulses of light were traveling. It reminded me of animated movies I've seen about the activity of neurons in the brain. But then, as my brain struggled to make sense of what I was seeing, the perspective shifted. It now appeared as if we were all immersed in some fluid solution, with small packets of Light and energy moving between the various trees and bushes. I remember shouting out loud, "It's all chemistry!" I definitely had a sense of molecules of intention, meaning, love, and energy moving from one living form to another, interacting, stimulating the release of more molecules of Light, and so on. I was in the midst of a wholly different ecosystem of life and energy, one that was generating Light even as Light was being exchanged back and forth between all the participants.

This experience lasted for a few minutes, then gradually my human consciousness reasserted itself. I became myself once more. But the almost biological, chemical, even neurological-like aspects of the subtle environment around me were now indelibly fixed in my memory.

We are used to talking about subtle and spiritual realms as if they are supernatural, removed from the reality and messiness of the physical world. More often than not, we use mystical and religious imagery and language to describe these realms and their inhabitants with images and language that further separate us from them. If we draw upon one or another of the many esoteric and occult systems and traditions that have evolved over the millennia, we are likely used to thinking about the transcendent realms in hierarchical terms, with higher and lower "planes" or dimensions arranged like the layers on a wedding cake or the rungs of a ladder. In such a perspective, the physical earth is almost always at the lowest or next to the lowest point.

I have found through my over seventy-plus years of interaction with the subtle realms that mystical or religious terms don't really describe what I experience, nor does the traditional image of a "wedding-cake universe" with one realm piled on top of another in layers of hierarchically ascending goodness and Light. For me, the subtle realms are an ecology—Earth's "second" or "expanded" ecology. I find the language, metaphors, and images that best describe what I experience come from an ecological perspective, as well as from biology, chemistry, physics, and even geology and engineering!

This can be a novel perspective that may take some getting used to. Along with the idea of Gaia, the Earth, as a radiant star of life, this ecological view is central to how I approach partnering with spirit. Therefore, as we explore the ecosystem of the non-physical worlds together, I shall do my best to keep everything as clear and understandable as possible.

Gaia

My first memory of encountering Gaia as a distinct presence occurred many years ago in a vivid dream. In it, I was standing on the sidewalk in front of the house in Menlo Park, California, where I had lived with my parents when I was five years old, the year before we moved to Morocco. A wide driveway led from the street to a garage adjoining the house itself, and a narrow-paved walk curved between the driveway and the front door. That door was closed, but standing in front of it on a stoop was a large woman dressed in a flowing garment, similar to a Hawaiian muumuu. I felt a need to go into the house, but I knew that in order to do so, I would have to pass this woman.

I started walking down the driveway and onto the path that led to the front door. The closer I got to the woman, the more I realized that everything around me—the pavement of the driveway, the grass of the front lawn, the flowers in my mother's garden, even the house itself—were part of her flowing dress. It was as if she were some primal force out of which everything was emerging, the presence of the earth itself. I could feel the power emanating from her. Approaching her, I felt a tinge of apprehension, for I knew she could just absorb me into her gown, making me part of her.

As I reached her, she smiled and said, "Are you afraid of me? I could simply make you a part of me, you know," echoing the sudden fear I had felt in the presence of such a Power. But even as she asked me this question, I knew that I had nothing to fear. Instead, all my apprehension vanished, and I felt a flow of love to this Presence. I could feel her love back to me. Then she stepped aside, and the door opened, allowing me to enter the house. At which point, having metaphorically returned to my human world, I woke up.

At the time, I didn't say, "Oh, that was a dream of Gaia." I wasn't familiar with that term. But I knew clearly that I had encountered the spirit or soul of the earth. Since then, I've had other experiences of the Earth as a living being. In this, I stand squarely in an ancient animistic and holistic tradition shared by every indigenous culture in the history of humanity. Indeed, Western society for various historical and cultural reasons is an outlier here, one of the very few societies that does not view the Earth as a living organism.

This is not a philosophical or ideological position for me. It arises from many experiences of the subtle life of our planet. In this, I am like a naturalist describing a tree or an animal I've encountered in the wild. Gaia, the *anima mundi* or the soul of the world, is a real presence for me and has been for much of my life. Of course, perceiving the presence of Gaia and understanding just what that presence is, are two different things. Understanding Gaia is the work of a lifetime…and more.

Recognizing Gaia as a living being—a metaphysical organism— has given me a very different look at the physical and non-physical worlds and the relationship between them. Many religious and occult traditions see this relationship as layered, like a wedding cake or a stepladder, with the Source of Light at the very top and the physical world at the bottom, like this:

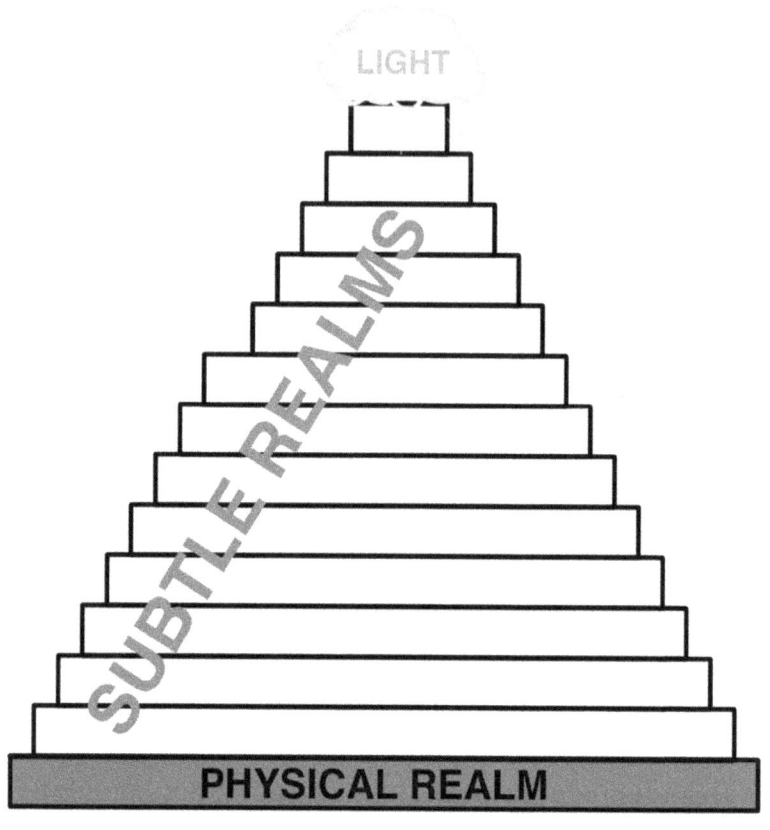

My experience is different. For me, the relationship between the physical world and the various subtle and spiritual realms is more organic and metabolic. For instance, if I were to see Gaia as a single cell, then the physical world and all the subtle realms are like organelles contained within the body of Gaia, each contributing a particular dynamic, a particular energy, a particular function to the cell as a whole.

My picture looks something like the following:

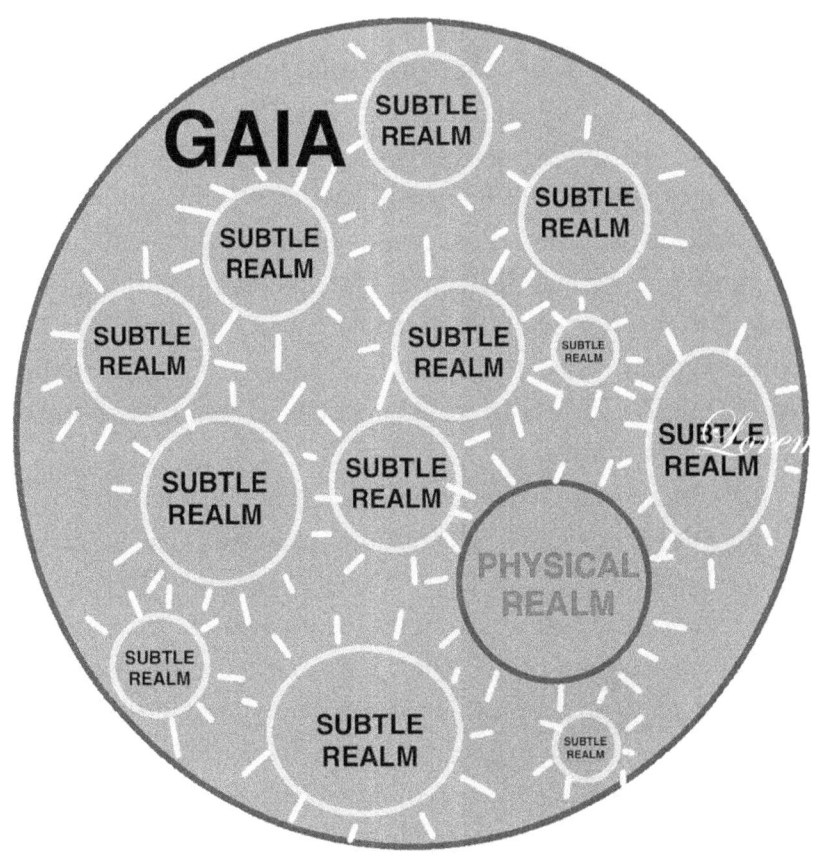

Here we see the physical world not at the bottom of a hierarchy of Light and energy but as one of many possible realms within which consciousness is evolving and through which Gaia is expressing. "Higher" and "Lower" are not terms that apply here. Instead, like the organelles in the body of a cell, each of these realms is interconnected, part of a larger whole, based on function and on the service each provides to the health and growth of that larger whole, as well as to each other. Each, including the physical realm, radiates its own frequency of Light and life, which becomes part of the radiance of Life emanating from Gaia as a star of Life. And each realm in turn is upheld and vitalized by the Light of

Gaia—the "cell"— as a whole.

This picture is a visual metaphor and oversimplifies the actual relational dynamics between the various realms that make up the whole body of Gaia as a planetary and spiritual organism. But it encourages us to think holistically, metabolically, and organically rather than hierarchically when trying to understand Gaia. And, it's important to understand as well that when we talk about different "realms" and the beings within those realms, including the physical realm, we are talking about different aspects and manifestations of Gaia as a star of life.

This is important when it comes to partnering with spirit. The partnerships that we will be considering all take place within the life and beingness of Gaia. Every being, whether physical or non-physical, including each of us, represents a living function within the body of Gaia as a whole. When we reach out to a subtle being, we are not only contacting a singular individual or a unique entity, but we are connecting to a manifestation of energy and life that is part of the metabolic dynamics and wholeness of Gaia.

This will, I hope, become clearer as we go along. But the essence of this perspective can be said this way: When we engage with anyone or anything, in this world or beyond it, we are also engaging with Gaia.

The Two Ecologies

Growing up, I was aware that everything in the world around me, whether it was a stone, a sofa, a chair, a plant, an animal, or another human being, emanated an invisible field of vital energy. It felt to me like everything was alive and possessed of a deep sentience. From time to time, this invisible field would open up or extend itself in a way difficult to describe, and I would be aware that beyond the physical world, another world existed, one that was home to what I perceived as beings of Light. These beings, when I would see them, seemed perfectly capable of interacting with the energy fields around physical phenomena. Occasionally, one of them would pause in whatever it was doing and look my way, and I would feel a wave of love coming from it to me. Now, I recognize that what I was seeing were likely nature spirits, but at the time, I thought they were angels as that was the only word I knew for non-physical beings of Light and spirit.

What was important was that I thought of them not as supernatural phenomena or as something out of the ordinary. To the contrary, they seemed an integral part of the natural world, part of the way things are. They seemed ordinary in that they blended organically into the environment around them, albeit the energy side of that environment.

Though I didn't know this word for it then, these beings seemed part of the ecology of the world.Later, when I was older and became aware of the term *ecology* and what it meant, I found it helpful to think of Gaia as possessing two interconnected ecologies, one physical and one subtle. They interact with each other across an energetic threshold that shares qualities of both.

Indeed, the two ecologies of the earth permeate each other since they are an integral part of the wholeness of Gaian, as we have seen.

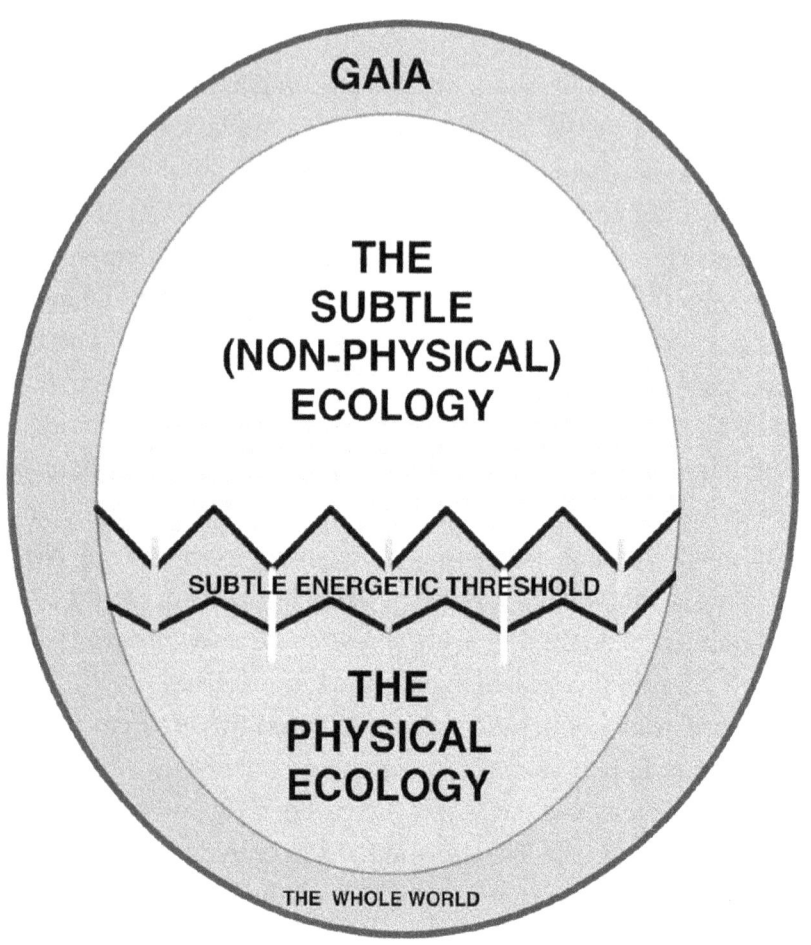

Looked at this way, the non-physical half of the earth represents the totality of the subtle and spiritual realms or dimensions (or "organelles," using the previous metaphor) of Gaia, whereas the physical half is, well, its physical body. In this, the planet possesses the same basic structure in macrocosm as we do in microcosm. For we, too, are beings with both subtle and material parts.

Ecology is the study of the interactions and relationships between organisms and their environment. It's easy to see this in the physical world; we're used to thinking of cells, bacteria, plants, and animals as organisms. We're organisms, too. But is an angel an organism? Is a nature spirit an organism? Is a non-physical person an organism?

An organism is usually defined by attributes such as possessing a metabolism (a way of processing energy), being able to grow and to respond to stimuli, adapting to its environment, and possessing an ability to communicate through various means. We can easily see how this definition and these properties apply to biological entities. But what about a being whose "body" is essentially energy of one kind or another or is made of something altogether different, neither matter nor energy, a substance for which the only name we have at the moment is "spirit" or "Light"? Is an angel alive? Is a nature spirit an organism?

From my point of view, the answer is yes.

Many of the subtle organisms of which I have been aware have been human, individuals who at some time in the past have passed out of the physical plane and into the subtle realms, as we all do eventually. Some, though, have been non-human, and these can take a multitude of forms. Just as the physical biosphere ranges from single-celled creatures all the way up to complex organisms like trees, roses, cats, elephants, and whales, so the subtle worlds have a similar diversity of beings. There are tiny, very simple beings that, as far as I can tell, live in the walls of my house and are part of the etheric or non-physical structure of the wood, stone and plaster, and there are vast landscape angels and devas, some of which encompass hundreds or even thousands of square miles of territory within their auras and consciousnesses.

All of these subtle beings possess the ability to sustain themselves. They can hold and process subtle energies, spirit, or Light within themselves, transforming it from one state to another: Thus, they have a metabolism, however different it may be from a biological one. They also maintain balance and coherency within themselves and in relationship to their surroundings: Thus, they exhibit homeostasis. They have a capacity to grow, they can respond to stimuli, they can adapt to their environment (though not through natural selection), and in some cases, they can reproduce, though again not in any biologically recognizable fashion. And they can certainly communicate.

Thus, the subtle worlds are filled with non-biological organisms, all of whom have interactions and connections with the particular environment or environments in which they operate. In short, the subtle worlds are an ecosystem unto themselves, Earth's "second ecology."

The Incarnational Biome

We are also subtle energy and spiritual biomes, or mini-ecosystems. There are many ways in which our incarnational totality can be mapped, depending on different religious, esoteric, or occult traditions and descriptions. Based on my own experiences, I find a tripartite description to be the simplest and most useful. Thus, I see each of us as possessing a physical body (with its psychological counterpart), a subtle energy body, and an encompassing soul body. Each of these is a biome or mini-ecosystem in its own right, each is connected to the other, and each is part of a larger environment from which it draws sustenance and connection to the larger whole of Gaia. Taken altogether, these three comprise our unique incarnational biome within the Gaian ecology. Here's a picture:

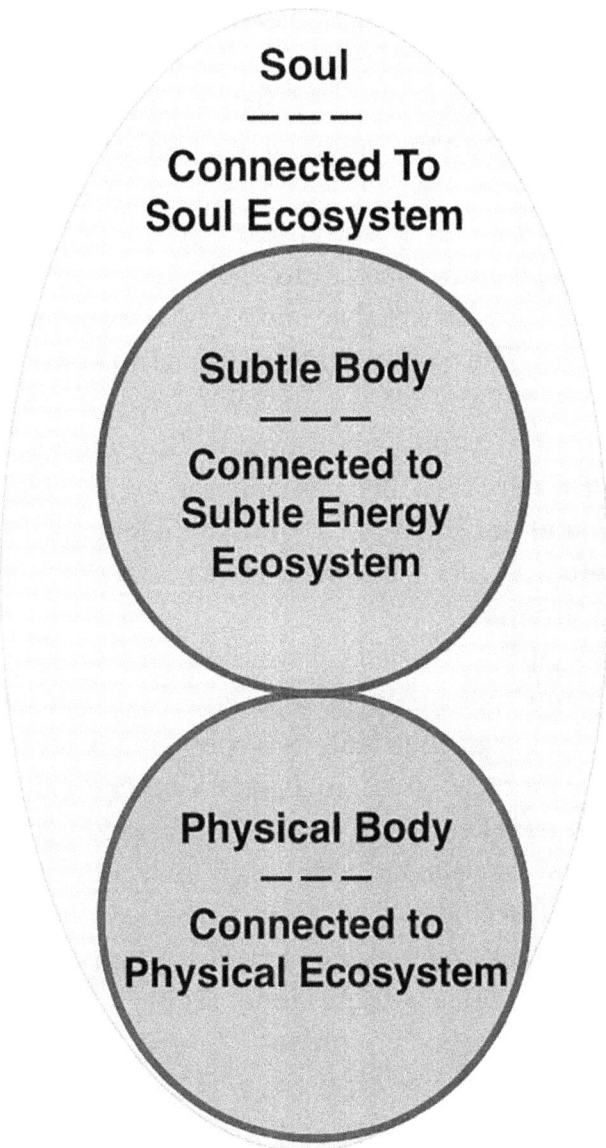

One way to think of ourselves is that we are each an integrated system that can both generate energy and be a conductor of energy. The first instance is why I use the image of being a star. A star generates energy out of its internal nuclear processes which it shares with the cosmos. We do something analogous. The incarnational processes that unite soul, subtle, and physical bodies into an integrated wholeness which are embedded within Gaia's wholeness, generate a spiritual energy that is unique to each of us. I call this our "Self-Light."

Through our daily activities, our thinking, and our feelings, we generate many different kinds of subtle energies that radiate out from us to become part of our subtle energetic environment. The quality of our thoughts and emotions and our actions determines whether what we radiate blesses or pollutes our subtle environment. But underneath this personality activity is the emanation of our Self-Light as an expression of our soul's incarnational intentions, the gifts it brings into the world, and the love that is at the foundation of our incarnation.

Think of Self-Light as a candle flame within us and ourselves, our personalities, as a lantern surrounding that flame. If the glass of the lantern is sooty and obstructed, the light of the candle is obscured. If, on the other hand, the glass of the lantern is kept clear, clean, and transparent, then that candle flame is revealed and magnified, illuminating the environment around us. The candle flame is always there. Our job is to keep the lantern clean, that is, to align our thoughts, feelings, and actions with this inner Light.

In this way, our thoughts, feelings, and actions can obscure or enhance our Self-Light, which is a spiritual energy that fosters and produces wholeness. The more we align (usually through love) with thoughts, emotions, and actions that promote wholeness, the greater the radiance of our Self-Light, the more we add to the wholeness in our environment, and the more connected we become to the Light within Gaia.

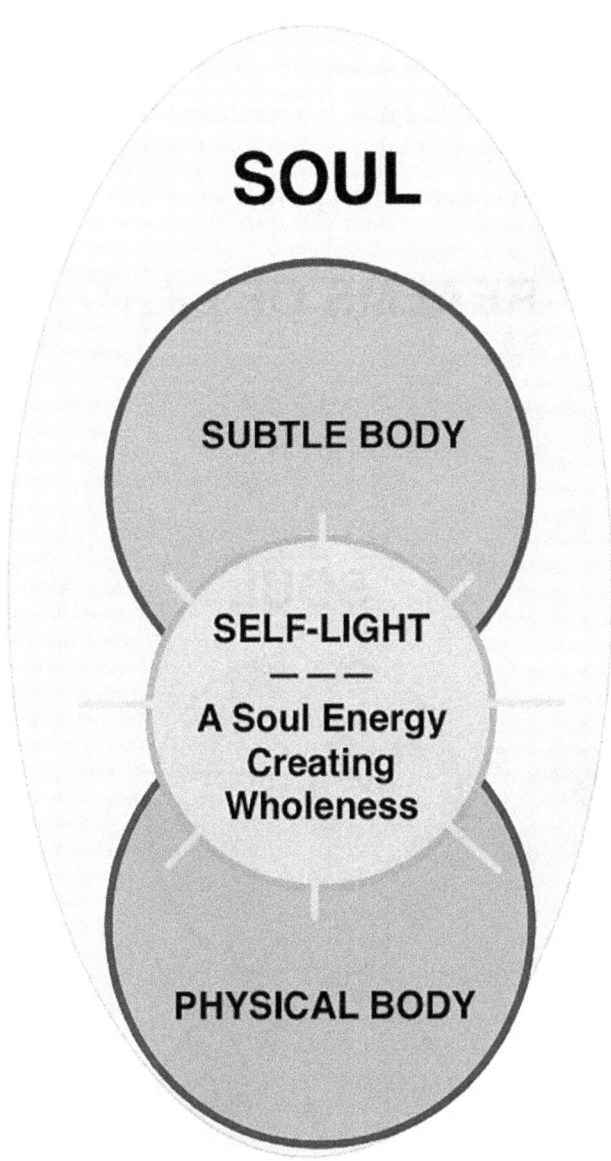

In addition to generating a unique spiritual energy to add to our world, we can also learn to attune to and partner with forces of Light operating in the "higher" or more complex and powerful realms of Light and energy within Gaia. How we do this we'll discuss later in this book. However, the realization that we *can* do this, that we can be a link in a process by which vital spiritual energies can enter and bless the physical world, is important to having a whole picture of our incarnational potential, a potential that is realized through the kind of partnerships we form with spirit.

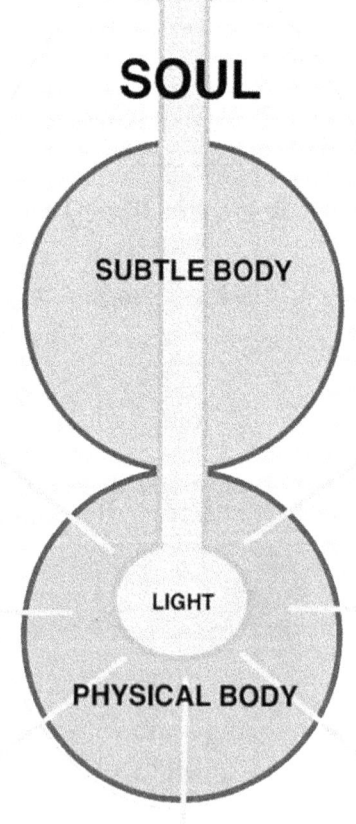

An Energy Metabolism

Whether we are generating Light or being a conduit for its transmission, we are participating in the energy metabolism of Gaia as a living being. We are a participant in that metabolism much as a cell is a participant in the metabolism of our body. Like a cell, we are designed for this participation. Unlike a cell, however, we can choose how much or how little to participate, at least up to a point. Physically, we can never completely sever our connection with and dependency upon Gaia without killing ourselves. We breathe Gaia's air. We eat food that comes from Gaia. Our bodies depend on the energy that Gaia provides. However, we can and do separate our consciousness from Gaia. We can think, feel, and act in ways that sever our sense of connectedness from Gaia. We live in a society that routinely acts at cross-purposes to the planet's metabolism, and we are suffering the consequences. The climate crisis is only one extreme example of these consequences.

It is time to realize that we are each an organism of energy and consciousness embedded within a larger organism of energy and consciousness. It's time to align these two so that they empower and enrich each other in synergy.

One way of doing this is through forming partnerships with spiritual and subtle beings.

We think of a partnership as a relationship between two or more beings working together toward a common goal. But when dealing with the subtle dimensions, it's more than that. It's a means of consciously creating connections that permit and enhance the flow and exchange of living, vital energies within the body of Gaia; whatever else it may be or achieve, each partnership with spirit is a participation in Gaia's energy metabolism. It is a conduit, a linkage, through which the life of Gaia may flow.

Three Stages

My experience of partnership with Gaia has gone through three stages. As I have mentioned, when I was a child, I was aware of an aura or emanation of energy coming from the things around me. I could feel it with animals and plants, but I could also feel it with inanimate objects, such as stones, or the furniture in my house. I had no idea what this energy was, except that sometimes it was very welcoming and loving, and other times, it could be repellant. I remember clearly when I was six years old, we were living in a house in Palo Alto across the street from a hospital where my mother worked as an RN. The house next door was a pleasant, ordinary-looking house, but to me, it gave off an energy that was dark and scary. I remember hurrying past it on the sidewalk when I would go out, half-concerned that something—I had no idea what—in that house would try to "get me."

Feeling the subtle life within the things around me, I began thinking of them as people. In my heart, I would acknowledge this life and would send it love. To my delight, I could often feel a loving energetic response back. For me, the entire world was alive, an experience that I think many children have.

As I recount in my memoir, *Apprenticed to Spirit,* when I was seven, I had a mystical awakening to and blending in unity with my soul. At that time, I experienced the process of how my soul incarnated as David Spangler, giving me insights that were invaluable when, some fifty years later, I began developing Incarnational Spirituality. The effect of this experience was that I became aware of a group of subtle and spiritual beings who were intimately involved as a support system for my incarnation.

Then in 1965, at the advice and urging of this inner support group, I left the university where I had been studying to become a molecular biologist and moved to Los Angeles to begin my life's work as a spiritual teacher. At that time, also as described in *Apprenticed to Spirit*, I was contacted by a subtle colleague whom I named "John." John became my partner and mentor for the next twenty-five years. Under his tutelage, I began expanding my contacts in the subtle and spiritual realms and began working with a variety of spiritual partners, particularly in the development of Incarnational Spirituality.

Thus, looking back over my life, I can see that my engagement with the subtle dimensions has gone through three stages, each becoming the foundation of the one that followed. The first is the loving engagement with the subtle life in the environment around me; I call this the "Blessing Partnership." The second is connection with an incarnational support group I think of as my natural allies or natural partners. The third stage is with the various inhabitants of the subtle ecology in service to Gaia. These levels of engagement will be described more fully later in this book.

PART II: THE BLESSING PARTNERSHIP

The blessing partnership is a partnership between one's Self-Light and the Light within the things that make up the environment around oneself. For instance, as I write this, I am in a room with two sofas, two chairs, four tables, some lamps, a television set, a footstool, a fireplace, and a colorful collection of pillows on the sofas. There is a carpet under my feet, and above me, there are beams on the ceiling. There are also plants of various kinds. Every one of these items contains within itself what I think of as an "incarnational seed of sacredness," a subtle energetic life that is, as all life is, in a process of development and evolution. For a complete description of this "seed" and of the life within inanimate artifacts, please see my book, *Techno-Elementals*.

Each life, each "seed" of sacred potential, is connected to the life and Light of Gaia. It is nurtured and vitalized by the flow of subtle energies within the environment, part of the energy metabolism of Gaia. Thus, each of the items in my room is a point of connection with—and a manifestation of—Gaia. Each of these items is a point of evolution of Gaian life.

As incarnate humans, we are also a part of the energy metabolism of Gaia (whether we're conscious of this or not). As we have seen, we generate subtle energies of various kinds, of which the one relevant to our discussion here is our Self-Light, an energy of blessing that fosters wholeness. By deliberately sharing our Self-Light with the things in our environment, we enter into a blessing partnership with our environment—and thus with Gaia, as well.

How do we do this?

Essentially, it is through consciously acknowledging and appreciating the subtle life within each of the objects around us and embracing that life in our love. We are extending our Self-Light as a vitalizing, stimulating, empowering, loving presence and force towards the Light and life within the things in our environment, just as we would extend our love and blessing to another person.

THE BLESSING PARTNERSHIP
THE FOSTERING OF LIGHT IN THE WORLD

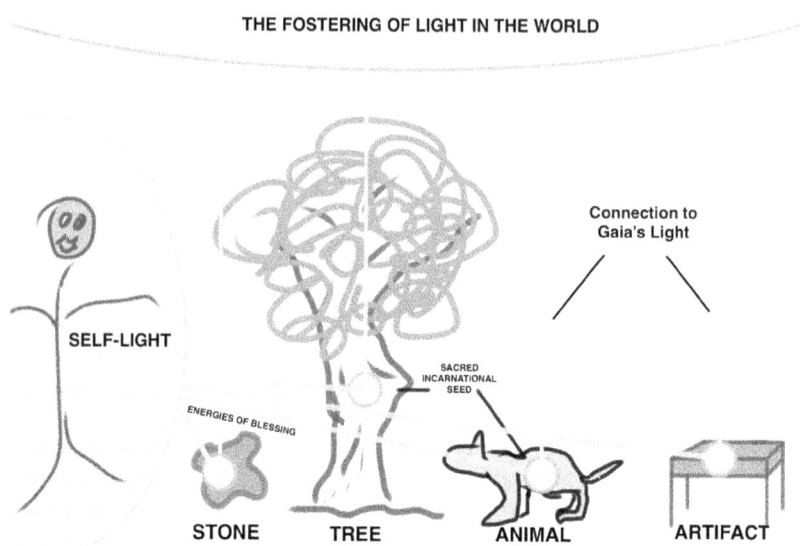

Here are a series of exercises from Incarnational Spirituality that may be helpful as suggestions of ways to proceed with this blessing partnership. Feel free to use them as written or to use them as models in designing your own exercises that fit your style and approach.

Self-Light

Here are two exercises for visualizing and attuning to one's Self-Light.

Self-Light Exercise 1

- Imagine a spiritual star at the center of the earth. It's a green star radiant with the power of planetary life. Imagine the light from this star rising up through the earth, surrounding you, bathing and nurturing the cells of your body, and forming a chalice around you.
- Imagine a spiritual star within the sun in the sky. It's a golden star radiant with the power of cosmic life. Imagine the light from this star descending from the heavens and pouring into the chalice of earthlight that surrounds you and fills your cells.
- Where the green and golden lights of these two stars meet in you, a new star emerges, a radiant star of Self-Light, born of the blending of the individual and the universal, the planetary and the cosmic, the physical and the spiritual, Soul and Earth. Here two great forces, Cosmos and Earth, are blended by the love and will of the soul acting at the heart of your incarnation.
- This Self-Light is constantly being generated by the deep processes of your incarnation. You can obscure it, but you cannot extinguish it. It surrounds you and fills you, always there for you to recognize and acknowledge, attune to and enhance with your attention and intention to let it shine upon the earth. You are a radiant, generative Source of Self-Light within a pillar of spiritual energy rising from the earth and Gaia and descending from the cosmos and soul.

- Take a moment to feel the generative star of this Self-Light within and around you. It is your connection to the earth, your connection to the cosmos, your connection to your own unique and radiant Self. Take a deep breath, drawing this Light into and throughout your body; breathe out, sending this Light out into your world. Filled with this Light of Self, attuned to heaven and earth, go about your day as a star of blessing.

Self-Light Exercise 2

- Let your attention and consciousness move into what you experience as the center of your body. This might be your heart; it might be some other area. Feel yourself surrounded by the millions and millions of cells whose individual lives make up your life. Feel the power and wonder of those lives all blending and connecting to support your own. You are immersed in a community of life.
- Feel the force and Light of a presence that pervades this community, drawing it into unity, giving it one identity. This presence is you. It is the presence of your Self. It makes you one being, one identity. Its light fills all your cells and all the activities that unite them.
- Let your attention and consciousness move more deeply into this presence, like moving into a sphere of Light that radiates the energy that forms into your physical body. Just rest in this Light of your unique Self. What does it feel like?
- When you are ready, let your attention move more deeply into this Light, as if you are moving toward the Source of this Self-Light. As you do so, you become aware

of a deeper Light that holds and empowers your Self-Light. This is the Incarnational Light itself and it emanates from the presence of your soul and the sacredness from which it comes. Through this Light of Incarnation, you are part of the community of the cosmos, the community of all incarnation, part of all that is. It is the root of who you are, but it does not consume you. You are an emergent form of that Incarnational Light, bringing creative potential and discovery into the universe.

- You are a gift of the Incarnational Light to the cosmos, and your Self-Light is the radiance of that gift.

- When you are ready, let your awareness and attention move from this deep Light into the radiance of your Self-Light. Feel the wonder and magic of being who you are, manifesting a unique and powerful will-to-be. Feel your lineage with the Light that runs through all creation and the way you individuate it.

- Feel your Self-Light permeating and uniting the presence of all your cells. Feel the wonder of your physical incarnation, of your mind and heart, your ability to think, feel, and to make choices. Feel the wonder of your spirit. Let yourself be filled and surrounded by this Self-Light.

- Standing in this Self-Light, go forth to meet your day.

Touch of Love

Touch of Love is a one-on-one partnership between you and a particular item in your environment. As the name suggests, it is facilitated by physical touch. I have found this an incredibly useful exercise, both in connecting to the subtle life and Gaian presence in my environment and in anchoring and stabilizing my own energy field when I have felt under stress or discombobulated for some reason energetically.

Here is an exercise to explore and experience this partnership.

Touch of Love Exercise

- Fill yourself with your Self-Light and with a felt sense of lovingness. You might imagine, for instance, your heart overflowing with love or your spine glowing with love. Express the highest form of love that you can authentically feel in your whole being—body, mind, heart, energy, and soul—right now.
- Feel this love flowing out from the core of your being, down your arms and into your hands. Feel this love pooling in your fingertips.
- Reach out and touch something. As you do so, feel the love in your fingertips overflowing. In this Touch of Love, you do not take anything into yourself. You do not really project it into anything either. You simply let it pool in your fingertips and overflow, allowing that which you touch to absorb it in its own way.
- As love flows through your touch, it also stirs and flows and circulates through your own being, bringing love to all parts of yourself just as you are bringing it to the things you touch.
- Likewise, as love flows through your touch, it also stirs and flows and circulates through your environment, rippling out in waves from the things you touch, expanding the influence of your loving touch.
- Feel this expanding, circulating love bringing the blessing and empowering vitality of your Self-Light into your environment.
- When you feel finished, just remove your fingers and

allow the love to be absorbed into all parts of your body.

We touch each other's incarnations all the time. The energies we project to each other, the way we think of each other, the feelings we surround others with, the looks we give, the tones of voice, the words we use; all of these are touches. But are they touches that help us to incarnate and help the incarnation of another, or do they hinder and obstruct? That is what only we can determine. We can remember, though, that a silent partnership of blessing is always at our real—and virtual—fingertips.

Grail Space

I use the term "Grail Space" to mean any space that holds sacredness, just as in legend the Holy Grail held the transformative blood of Christ. Sacredness in this instance manifests as the incarnational consciousness and process that brings creation into being and sustains it in its unfoldment.

We all live in Grail Space. The entire cosmos is the primal Grail Space holding the sacredness of the Generative Mystery which I call the Sacred. But this primal Grail Space can be accentuated in local space at any time we invoke the presence and flow of sacredness by honoring the incarnational process through which it manifests.

The practice of creating a local Grail space is one of standing in our own Self-Light and engaging the local environment around us to evoke more fully the Life and Light that flows from the primal Grail Space, i.e., from the Sacred itself. Fundamentally, this is a practice of connecting through presence and love with everything around us. It is an act of honoring and loving our environment, inviting the life within it to respond energetically and express its own Grail capacities. It is the act of mutual holding that turns the environment, with ourselves in it, into a Grail in which sacredness may shine forth.

The creation of Grail Space is a reciprocal act, not something we do to anything else. It is an act of extending an invitation, allowing the environment to respond as fully as it can in the moment. Grail Space is born of relationship and mutual engagement based on honoring the sovereignty and identity of all involved.

Creating Grail Space is a simple process, but I break it down into a number of steps just so you can get a sense of the procedure. To read the exercise, it can seem like a lot, but it's really a very fast, simple process. The main difference between this technique and simply sending love into your environment is the act of honoring and connecting with the identity of everything about you in a partnership. It is not you doing something to the things in your environment. It is you joining with them in collaboration to create a mutually beneficial space or field out of which sacredness may emerge.

One way to think of this is as if everything in your environment is a person and you are joining hands with them to form a great circle. This circle creates the Grail Space, and into it, sacredness is invoked.

Grail Space Exercise

- Begin by standing in your own Sovereignty, in the felt sense of your unique identity and your connection to your soul and to the sacred. If you wish, you can imagine this Sovereignty as a "spine" of Self-Light within you, an axis around which your physical and subtle bodies develop and align.

- Imagine this spine of Self-Light becoming brighter and brighter as it unfolds from the love within your Soul and within the Sacred of which it is a part. As this Self-Light becomes brighter within you, it expands and enfolds you.

- Imagine yourself standing in an oval of Self-Light emanating from your "spine" of Sovereignty and individuality, an oval that surrounds you on all sides, top and bottom, connecting you with the energies of the world. It forms and radiates from you as a personal Grail, an incarnational field holding sacredness.

- Everything in your immediate environment is an expression of the Sacred. Everything you see participates in the primal Grail Space. Everything has within itself a "spine" of incarnational intent and Light, its own form of Sovereignty and identity. Imagine yourself surrounded with a multitude of "grails of Light" emanating from everything in the space around you. In your heart, acknowledge and give honor to the presence of all these "spines" or "grails" of incarnational and sacred Light.

- Imagine your aura of Self-Light—your internal, personal Grail of Sacredness and Incarnational Light—expanding into the room, joining in love with the myriad multitude of Lights all around you, inviting them into an alliance and collaboration with you. Feel your Light augmenting and blending with the Lights around you, feel their Lights blending with and augmenting your own. You are forming a subtle partnership with your environment, and everything seen and unseen within it. Feel this partnership turning your immediate, local environment into a Grail that you and all the things around you collaborate to create, a Grail you share.

- The felt sense of this partnership and the field of reciprocal energy that generates it is the Grail Space. It is a field of collaborative partnership and support in the incarnational process with everything around you in your local space, a partnership and fellowship that can receive and hold a Presence of sacredness, a presence of Gaia.

• Standing in this Grail Space, acknowledge this Presence of sacredness heightened in yourself and your environment. Imagine it being held in this space, doing whatever it needs to do to foster wholeness and well-being, and then overflowing into the larger world beyond - a source of energy, blessing, love, and life.

• Stay in this Grail Space as long as feels comfortable. When you feel tired or restless, simply draw your Self-Light back into yourself, giving thanks to your energy partners for their participation. Imagine their incarnational light moving back into themselves as well, knowing the environment you share will resonate with the Light and Presence you have collectively invoked for as long as it is able.

• Stand in your Sovereignty, acknowledging your wholeness, your integrity, your identity, and your connection to the Sacred. Then go about your daily affairs.

The preceding are simple exercises through which you can embody and express a blessing partnership with the environment around you and the subtle life it holds. You can do the same thing at any time simply by acknowledging the life in the things around you and asking that life be blessed in its evolutionary journey. You can hold the things around you in your love and goodwill. You can acknowledge the presence of Light and of Gaia's Life in the world you share. As much as anything, it is your attitude to the things around you that can form—or dissolve—a blessing partnership.

Engaging in a blessing partnership with your environment

is the simplest, easiest form of partnering with spirit. It is a place to begin, a place to practice your Self-Light and your energetic participation in the life and metabolism of Gaia. For when you radiate a loving energy into your environment, you are enhancing the flow of vitality and life within the body of Gaia. You are a presence of empowerment just as the great planetary angels and Devas are presences of empowerment for the environments that they overlight. This is a rich service anyone can offer - a participation in Gaia that is open to anyone who is willing to open their hearts and minds to the living world around them.

PART III: OUR NATURAL ALLIANCES

There are different ways we can describe the incarnational process through which the soul becomes part of the incarnate physical world. The simplest—and least accurate—description is that the soul simply enters and takes over a body much the way a driver enters and takes over an automobile. In my experience, the process is more complex. If we accept that Gaia is itself a complex organism possessing a metabolism and physiology based on the interaction of spiritual and subtle energies and that this metabolism and physiology creates a holistic, interconnected internal ecology, then incarnation is a matter of engaging, connecting, and integrating with that complexity.

The following picture illustrates what I mean. Although undoubtedly an oversimplification, I have found it useful to describe the soul's incarnational connections as occurring in four interrelated domains. There are connections to the natural world on the one hand and to the collective field of human consciousness and activity on the other; providing a "horizontal" axis. The "vertical" axis is between the forces of individuation which give rise to a unique human individuality and personality and the forces of the "transincarnational" and subtle realms. In this picture, I list just a few of the possible "players" or needed points of connection and engagement within each of these four quadrants. The soul creates an embodied field that is "holopoietic" (wholeness-creating) that attracts and synthesizes the various connections that it needs to give form and substance to its incarnate self. These connections enable it to be part of nature, part of humanity, expressive of an individual personhood while also remaining attuned to the transpersonal and transcendental—i.e., transincarnational—dimensions of Gaia. The function of the soul is to weave all these connections into a coherent and integrated wholeness.

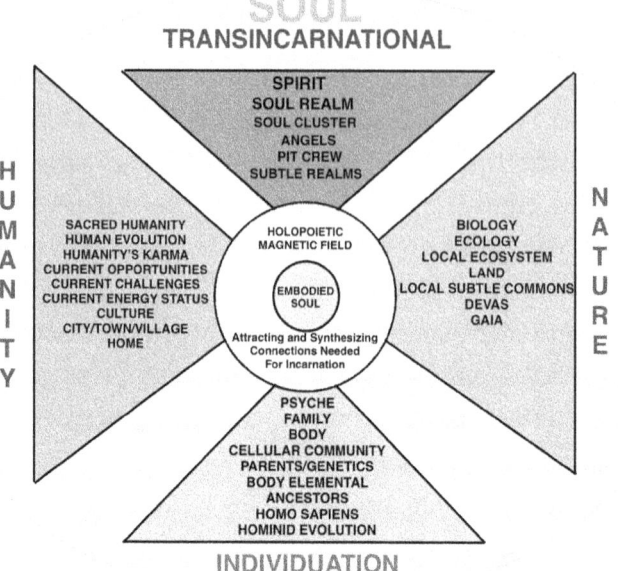

Presence

This integrative weaving can be seen as a two-step process. The first step is internal. It is something the soul does drawing on its own love, wisdom, experience, and intention. It creates a holopoietic ("wholeness-creating") magnetic field, reaching into the four primary energy fields of Gaia with which it needs to connect: Nature's energy field, Humanity's energy field, the energy field of personal Individuation, and the Transincarnational energy field of the subtle and spiritual worlds, including the realm of the soul.

This holopoietic field is the presence of the soul's intent, love, and spiritual power within the incarnate world. I call it our Presence. It is a vitally important element in partnering with spirit, though its full role will be more evident in the later chapters of this book.

Here is a picture showing this relationship:

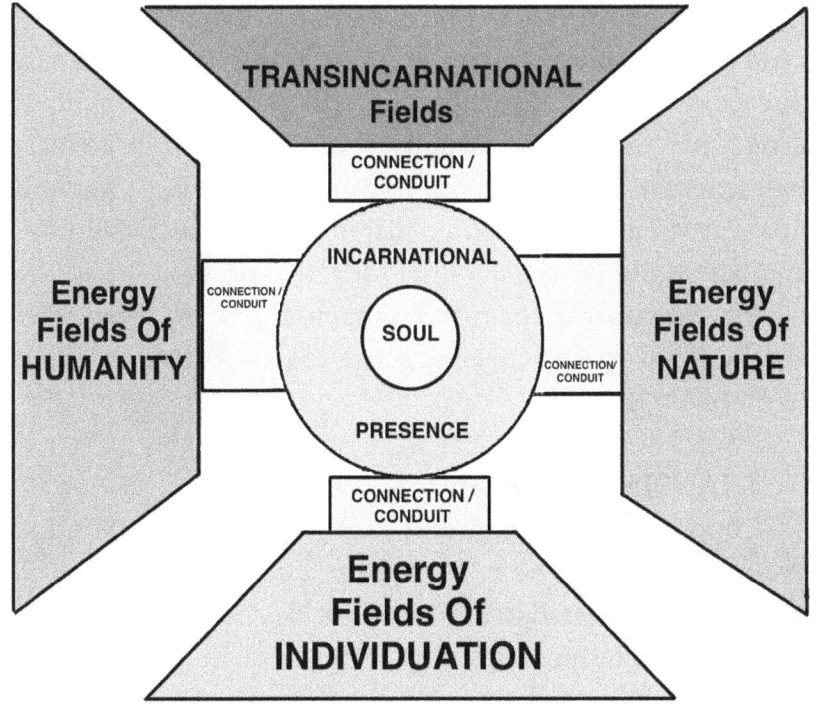

Attuning to your Presence and making it part of your life is an essential practice within Incarnational Spirituality. Here is the exercise for making this attunement.

Presence Exercise

<u>Important note</u>: In part of this exercise, you are asked to attune to your everyday personal self. This is not an exercise in judgment or self-criticism. There may be things you don't like about yourself, are ashamed of, and wish to change or improve. That is perfectly fine, but that perception is not part of this particular exercise. You may certainly make an honest appraisal of yourself; indeed, this is essential. But do not get into self-blame or criticism or begin listing ways in which you can change and do better. That is another kind of work, one you can engage in at another time.

Find a comfortable place to stand. This is a moving exercise, one in which you will be turning to face the four directions. In each direction you will face and attune to an aspect of yourself, eventually drawing them all into the wholeness of your Presence. If you are unable to move in this way for any reason, then just imagine yourself standing and turning to face each of the four directions.

Imagine yourself in a sacred or magical circle, a protected and honored space—an emergence space—that is dedicated to this exercise.

TRANSINCARNATIONAL

Choose any direction and face it. In this direction is a vision of your Soul, your "Transincarnational" Self, the part of you that is connected to the inner worlds and to transcendent states of communion and unity, spirit and creativity. Take a moment to reflect on being part of Spirit, part of a vast ecology of life and consciousness not limited to physical reality. What does this mean to you? What energy does it carry for you? What do you feel in its presence? What is your felt sense of your transpersonal nature? Be honest in your appraisal.

Take a moment to honor your Soul and Transincarnational Self. Appreciate it, and give it thanks for its contribution to the wholeness of who you are. It is a channel through which Sacredness—your sacredness—can flow and act. Embrace it with your love.

NATURE

Turn ninety degrees and face a new direction. In this direction is a vision of your Nature Self, your World Self, your Earthiness, the part of you that is connected to Gaia, to the physical world, and to nature as a whole. Take a moment to reflect on being part of this world, part of the biosphere, part of the realm of physical matter, part of the Earth. This part of you connects you to the World Soul. It connects you to ecology, to nature, to plants and animals everywhere. It connects you to the land, to seas and mountains, plains and valleys, swamps and deserts. What does this mean to you? What energy does it carry for you? What do you feel in its presence?

Take a moment to honor your Nature self. Appreciate it, and give it thanks for its contribution to the wholeness of who you are. It is a channel through which Sacredness—your sacredness—can flow and act. Embrace it with your love.

INDIVIDUATION

Turn ninety degrees and face a new direction. In this direction is a vision of your Personal individuating Self. This includes your personality, your Body Elemental, and your genetic lineage, those things and experiences that make you unique in the world. Take a moment to reflect on this uniqueness as a person. Reflect on what defines you, and what makes you different from others. This is your ordinary, everyday self that connects you to the physical world around you. What does this mean to you? What energy does it carry for you? What do you feel in its presence? What is your felt sense of your Personal self? Be honest in your appraisal, but do not engage in self-criticism.

Take a moment to honor your Personal, everyday self. Appreciate it, and give it thanks for its contribution to the wholeness of who you are. It is a channel through which Sacredness—your sacredness—can flow and act. Embrace it with your love.

HUMANITY (OR SPECIES)

Turn ninety degrees and face a new direction. In this

direction is a vision of your Humanness, the part of you that connects you to the human species and to human culture, creativity, and civilization. Take a moment to reflect on being human. Your humanity gives you various attributes and potentials not shared by other creatures on this earth. Your humanness makes you part of a planetary community of other human beings, part of the spiritual idea or archetype of Humanity. What does this mean to you? What energy does it carry for you? What do you feel in its presence? What is your felt sense of your humanness? Be honest in your appraisal, but do not engage in self-criticism. Humanity may have its faults, and it may behave badly in the world, but that is not the focus here.

Take a moment to honor your Human self. Appreciate it, and give it thanks for its contribution to the wholeness of who you are. Being human is a channel through which Sacredness—your sacredness—can flow and act. Embrace it with your love.

PRESENCE

Turn ninety degrees back to the direction you were facing when you started. At this time, turn your attention to yourself at the center of these four "Selves," these four elements of your Incarnation, these four "fixed structures" within your subtle field: Your Personal self, your Human self, your Nature or Gaian self, your Transincarnational self. You are the point of synthesis where they all meet, come together, blend, partner, cooperate, merge, and co-create wholeness.

Feel the energies of these four selves, these four directions, flowing into and through you, blending, merging, and creating an open, evocative, creative space within you. Feel what emerges from this space. Feel the holistic Presence of your unique incarnation and sovereignty rising around you and within you, enfolding you, supporting you, becoming you. Feel the Presence that embraces, includes, grows out of, and is larger than the four selves you have acknowledged and honored.

Who are you as this Incarnational Presence? What is the felt sense of who you are?

At the same time, feel the love that honors and holds these four aspects of you and of the world together, enabling them to collaborate and work in partnership. This love is the fire of sacredness within you. Honor this and honor yourself for your ability to hold it in your Presence.

CLOSURE

Stay in the circle, feeling the reality and energy of your Presence for as long as feels comfortable to you. When you begin to feel restless, tired, or distracted, just give thanks. Give thanks to your wholeness, to your Presence, to the Sacredness from which it emerges, and which is represented within the ecology of your incarnate life. Absorb, integrate, and ground as much of the felt sense and energy of this Presence as you can or wish into your body, into your mind and feelings, into yourself. Then step forward out of your circle thus ending this exercise.

The soul does not have to undertake this integrative, connective, holopoietic process by itself. It has help. Specifically, it has help in each of the four quadrants. These are beings who become intimately associated with an incarnation; they are our organic natural subtle partners, our natural allies. They support the activity and energy of our Presence and are attuned to it.

Collectively, I call them our "Entelechy" (En-TELL-Eh-Key). They help connect our individual incarnational biome, our incarnate self, with the larger sphere of Gaia's energy metabolism (which includes all of nature and all of humanity as dynamic fields of energy and consciousness).

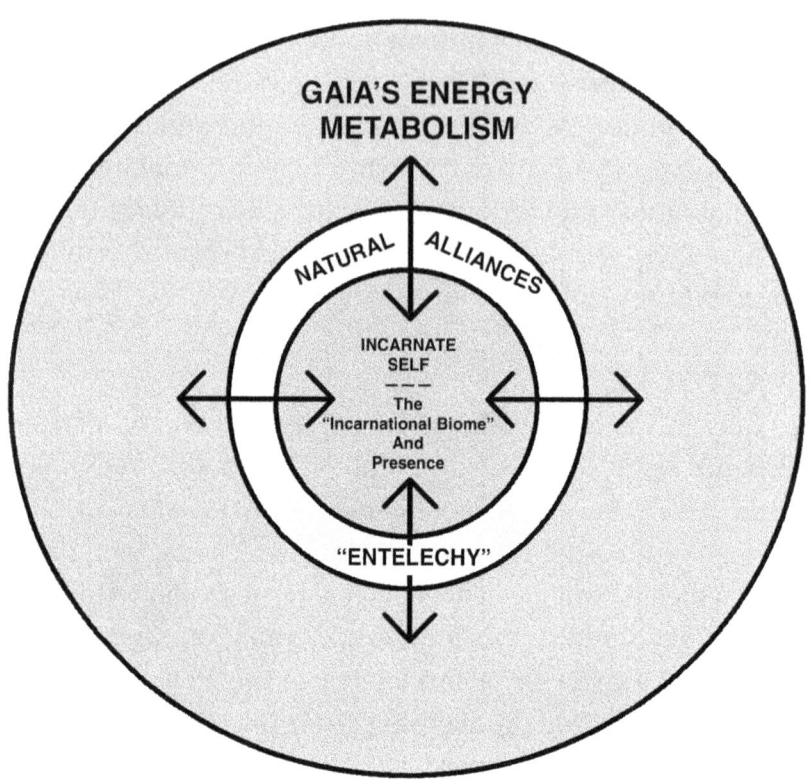

Over the years, I have identified certain specific beings who act as our natural allies in each of these four quadrants of incarnation. They are an Incarnational or "Body" Elemental; our Body Intelligence; our "Pit Crew;" and a Guardian Angel. They are associated with the same four quadrants as we just saw in the Presence exercise.

The Entelechy

The word *Entelechy* (or *entelecheia*) was invented by Aristotle to describe the motion of potentiality into actuality and manifestation that defines a being. My friend and colleague, the poet and scholar William Irwin Thompson, used the word to refer to a collection of subtle allies with whom he worked and with forces intimately engaged with co-creating a person's incarnation. I am using it similarly to refer to our natural allies, as collectively these beings work together to help bring the potentiality of an incarnation into actuality.

For the most part, these are allies for whose help we don't need to ask as they agreed before we ever took physical form to aid us as best they can. How effective their help can be depends a great deal on the choices we make and how we lead our lives. It's quite possible through negative thoughts, feelings, and actions to create an energetic barrier between the Entelechy and ourselves, a kind of energetic fog that can block or even in some cases repel their efforts and blessings. But even in such a case, they never abandon us. In some cases, such as with the Incarnational Elemental or the Body Intelligence or even more, the soul itself, they cannot, for they are intimately woven into the fabric of our incarnation.

Of course, if we are aware of them and deliberately seek to enhance the partnership with them through our conscious connection, this makes the involvement of our Entelechy even more powerful and present in our lives.

Entelechy has a further meaning. While each of our natural allies—the members and participants of the Entelechy—relate to us in their own specific ways, and together through their love and their intent to support us, they create a field of collaborative energy which is itself a supportive presence. In effect, the Entelechy as a whole field is itself another natural ally.

My experience of the Entelechy is that of an embracing and upholding presence of love. It's an interconnected network of subtle presences and intelligences dedicated to the manifestation and success of a person's incarnation. While I might attune to a specific natural ally for help or support in a particular situation—for instance, attuning to my Body Intelligence for help in healing some part of my body—attuning to the Entelechy gives me a generalized sense of being upheld and empowered. It surrounds me with a sense of being loved which in itself is a blessing as I go through my daily life. And if I'm faced with a situation in which I may not know which of my natural allies I can or should turn to for help, I can attune to the group field as a whole—the Entelechy—for partnership and assistance.

Attuning to the Entelechy

Here's a simple way to attune to the Entelechy, the combined, collaborative field of energy jointly created by your natural alliances.

- Take a moment to attune to each Natural Ally in its quadrant. Feel the felt sense, the sensations, of who or what this particular Ally is and how it relates to you and is supportive of you.
- Now attune to how they come together in a shared dedication to the success of you and your incarnation. Feel into the field created when they touch each other in mutual purpose and love. This is the Entelechy at the center of your natural alliances, uniting them as a supportive whole. What does this feel like to you? How does it embrace and hold you and your incarnation?
- At any time, whenever you need, you can attune to this collective field of support and love, in addition to attuning to a specific Natural Ally. It is always there for you, always part of your life.

Let's explore each of these four quadrants of the Entelechy—our Natural Alliances—in turn, beginning with the quadrant of Individuation and the Body Elemental.

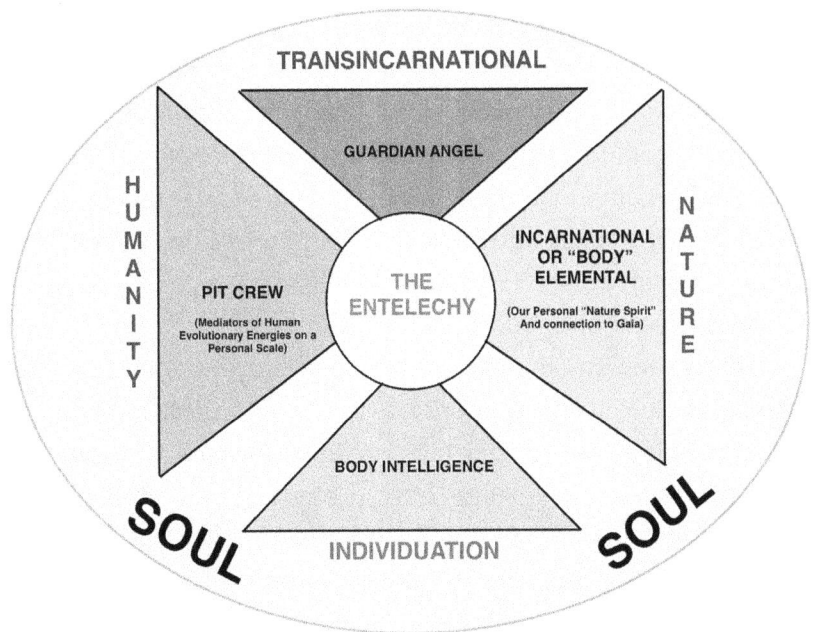

Individuation: The Body Intelligence

The body has its own collective intelligence and wisdom. Indeed, it possesses several layers of these. Each cell has its own subtle aspect, its own memory, its own link to Spirit. Similarly, organized collectives of cells working together for a single function - i.e., "organs" and "tissues" - have their own subtle aspect, memory, and link to Spirit. A liver, for instance, is not simply the collection of all liver cells working together but is an energetic and spiritual entity, one that emerges through synergy out of the interaction of the liver cells (and also out of the genetic plan of the human body which dictates there shall be a liver). At the next level, all the organs, tissues, and systems of the body collectively comprise an emergent intelligence/entity which is the Body Intelligence. It is the intelligence of the physical biome, our personal ecosystem.

But this is only part of the whole picture. The Body Intelligence also draws upon and is influenced by deep roots that extend into the past, into the ancestral and karmic (or instinctive and habitual) soil of its evolutionary history. One such root links the body to the primal forces and memories of Gaia and nature, right back to the archaic single-cell creatures that made the oceans of primeval Earth their home. Another root links to the memories and wisdom of hominid evolution, from which the human body emerged. There are roots that go back into racial and ethnic ancestors as well. And of course, there are the roots that extend from the genetic lineages and heritages of one's mother and father.

This means that the body's intelligence draws on millions of years of evolutionary experience, a deep biochemical, anatomical, and physiological wisdom that becomes focused through our parental and familial lineage into our physical individuality.

If we think of the Body Intelligence as a tree, then this deep root system is complemented by a "canopy of branches and leaves" that is uniquely our own. It might look something like this:

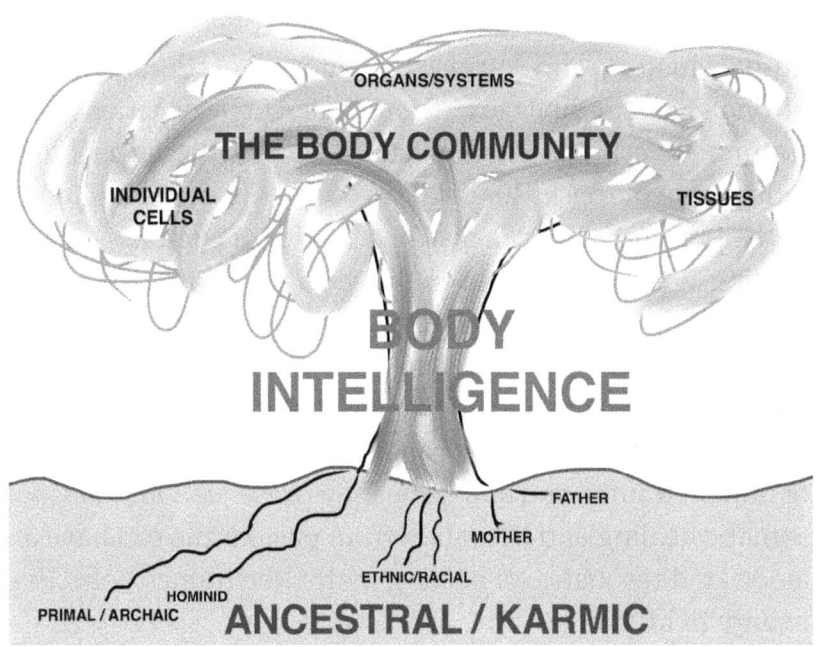

We are each a "body community" of cells and of the tissues, organs, and physiological systems they create. Each cell is a spiritual and physical intelligence in its own right. When they come together to form specific organs, these collectives give rise to an "intelligence of the organ," as well. Likewise, various organs and tissues may work together as a specific "system," like the circulatory system or the digestive system, which also has its unified intelligence. All of these together, in resonance with the ancestral roots, form the emergent sentient field that is the Body Intelligence as a whole.

This means that each of us has the ability to attune to our body as a whole, to a specific system within it, to the organs that participate in that system, or to the cells that make up that organ. In addition, we can attune to the deep ancestral wisdom arising from the evolutionary history of our body.

Unfortunately, the Body Intelligence also has roots in the memories of trauma and suffering that make up so much of human experience. Whether it's the collective trauma of human history and karma, the intergenerational trauma of one's genetic lineage—or one's personal experiences of trauma—the Body Intelligence can carry the impact and influence of the past. This can be a source of pain and limitation in the present, but it can also be a source of compassion and healing when one is able to draw on the innate spirit and Light within the Body Intelligence—and within the Entelechy as a whole—in order to transmute the effects of the trauma, whatever its origin. Our Body Intelligence can be a way in which the Light of our Soul can reach into the energetic layers of human trauma and add its healing presence. Our personal somatic healing and liberation from past karma can have an associated resonance of healing within the human collective energy field.

In this sense, we may think of the Body Intelligence as a vast library, or more accurately, as a community whose members can access a wide range of information.

The Body Intelligence is our closest subtle ally. It knows what it needs for health, for wholeness, for healing. That this knowledge is often ignored or overridden by our mental and emotional states and needs, or by the customs or habits of our surrounding culture, or by the effects of trauma, whether personal or collective, doesn't mean that the Body Intelligence isn't present and active, doing its best to keep us functioning. It only means that we may not fully avail ourselves of (or may even interfere with) its inner resources of attunement, wisdom, and balance.

The Body Intelligence is primarily focused on what is happening within and to the body. However, it is also fully aware of the subtle environment which surrounds it and is sensitive to the quality and nature of subtle energies that it encounters. In fact, although I'm describing the Body

Intelligence as if it were confined to the physical body, it would be just as accurate to say that it encompasses all the "bodies" through which we experience incarnation: mental, emotional, and subtle. Our Body Intelligence has a high degree of situational awareness that can help us live in harmony and safety with the world around us. This awareness can be ignored, dulled by distraction, or weakened by our lifestyle. However, if we pay attention to our body with love and respect, its intelligence is there to act as a natural ally.

I think of the Body Intelligence as being primarily concerned with the integrated and coherent operation of the physiology and metabolism of the body as a whole. It knows who needs to do what, when, where, and how so that our body functions smoothly as designed. It knows how to be a whole and healthy organism, which makes it a powerful ally when it comes to healing.

If I want to attune to the Body Intelligence, I direct my attention and awareness into my body itself as an intelligent presence. I don't expect it to communicate with me through words; its language is one of sensation and intuition. But your experience could be different from mine, so it is important to explore how you discern and encounter your Body Intelligence in your own unique way. However, I do recommend developing a practice of tuning into your body with love at least once a day and being open to listening to how it responds.

Nature: The Incarnational (Body) Elemental

The Incarnational Elemental is an important part of our incarnation. It is a partner to the soul in the formation of the physical body. Although integrated with the energy of our physical body, it is a separate entity. I think very early in the evolution of the hominid form, when humanity was part of the animal kingdom, this being developed from nature spirits or lesser Devas working with the evolution of our species. As we evolved a complex energy field, one capable of holding and expressing the higher frequencies of consciousness and soul, this "human nature spirit" or "human Deva" evolved along with us, becoming symbiotically aligned with our incarnate energy system. Our Incarnational Elemental helps to mediate the relationship between the soul and the subtle environment of the physical world.

The word *incarnation* means to take on flesh, something tangible and substantial. But it could also mean "taking on information," specifically the information that allows us to connect with and become part of a larger whole. For instance, I could be hired by a company and show up at the office to work, but if no one introduces me around to my co-workers and my boss and tells me how the company operates and what its goals are, then I'm not really there. I'm a body occupying space in the office, but I can't say I'm part of the company.

Think of the universe as filled with a spectrum of frequencies of life, energy, and consciousness. Each frequency attunes to a world of information, much like the dial on a radio tunes us into all the news, music, and talk shows being broadcast by a particular station. If I dial that station, I make a connection with all that information. I become part of that world, and it becomes part of me. But this wouldn't happen if I didn't have a radio or television to access that frequency.

The soul may possess within itself the ability to connect to and come into alignment with the incarnate realm (made up of the physical world and its subtle environment), but it doesn't necessarily have the information it needs to become a functional part of that realm or part of the collective human energy field as it exists at the moment of its conception and birth.

This is where the Incarnational Elemental comes in.

The Incarnational Elemental is the "radio" or "television" that helps the soul gain the information it needs for incarnation as it accesses the frequencies of physical, biological, and etheric Gaian life. It helps the soul to make connections with the energies that define this world. The Incarnational Elemental is our connection to the life and consciousness of Gaia.

Now, this is an overly simplistic way of describing this entity, and I wouldn't want to press the metaphor too far, but let's say that I want to cook a Greek dinner, but I don't have a recipe. I tune into a cooking channel—i.e., a frequency—on my TV that is offering "Lessons in Greek Cooking." I now have access to the information I need. But I still don't have my dinner. Listening to and watching this channel though, I discover the ingredients I need and how to put them together which allows me to cook the dinner. Now, I have my Greek meal. It is a tangible, physical reality, but it has emerged out of non-physical information mediated by my television.

The body is a tangible reality, but it emerges out of a blending of the soul's purpose, desire, energy, and will with a body of information held in the subtle domains—the "information space"—of the world. The Incarnational Elemental helps the soul access and connect to that information and in this way helps it manifest a body.

Sometimes I think of the Incarnational Elemental as akin to a concierge. It acts as an enabler and mediator between the soul and the physical world, just as a concierge is an interface between a hotel guest and the city they are visiting. It helps the soul attract and engage with what it needs for its "stay" in the "human hotel."

As I understand it, the Incarnational Elemental is drawn from a "pool" of such beings who are part of Gaia. As a "Body Angel" or "Body Deva," it works with the soul from conception onward, returning to its own domain when the body dies. It is an evolving entity with its own intelligence separate from our own that is dedicated to serving and helping our incarnational well-being at a physical level. It is attuned to a deep, Gaian wisdom built up over millennia of evolution and experience. It is a direct connection between ourselves as individuals and Gaia itself.

The Incarnational Elemental is deeply connected to the physical energy field of the body. It can be difficult to discern where the boundaries are between it and, say, the collective cellular intelligence of the body, the Body Intelligence. It is an ally seeking to promote our physical well-being and wholeness, and it operates, much as a nature spirit does, as a connective conduit between the energy of our body and the energy fields of the environment around us.

In working with healing, one may attune to and work with one or more of the body's energy fields. For example, one could work directly with the intelligence of an organ or of a cell, or with the etheric body. But calling upon the Incarnational Elemental as an ally is always a good practice.

The Body Intelligence I experience is a presence within me, one that acts across a spectrum from the intelligence within a single cell to that within particular tissues, organs, and the body as a whole. When I wish to attune to it, I turn my attention and listening to my body or to a specific part of my body depending on the attunement I am seeking. With the Incarnational Elemental, though, I have a sense of a presence that is around me and companioning me. I often visualize it as a sphere of intelligent energy and Light surrounding my body (though not to be confused with my aura, which is a different subtle energy phenomenon altogether and one reflection of my own state of being rather than that of the Incarnational Elemental). Then, I attune to that sphere of intelligence around me, sending it love for its service and its connection to Gaia as a whole, and, as always, listening to whatever promptings or feelings, intuitions, or insights may arise. I experience this presence as an embodiment of joy, Gaia's joy, in the presence and potentials of life.

For many years, I called this entity the "Body Elemental," which naturally created some confusion with the Body Intelligence. However, further research showed me that, whereas the Body Intelligence deals with the physical manifestation of an incarnation, the entity I'm now calling the Incarnational Elemental deals with a good deal more. It assists the soul with a wide range of connections between itself and Gaia and plays a role in the creation and development of the subtle body and the subtle energy field. Because it is an ally for the whole incarnational process, not just its physical aspects, I decided to call it the Incarnational Elemental.

Humanity: The Pit Crew

If the Incarnational Elemental represents our connection to Nature and Gaia, broadly speaking, then that field of intelligence, wisdom, and caring that I call our "Pit Crew" represents our connection to the overall collective energy field of Humanity.

Hillary Clinton famously wrote that "it takes a village to raise a child." The same could be said about an incarnation. None of us enters embodied life alone. There are always those individuals in the subtle and spiritual realms who accompany and watch over us, assisting where they are able and to the extent that they are able. They are energetically linked to our individual incarnation and require no special help to make that connection. This is why I think of them as natural allies.

These beings are there to help you express your humanity and to draw on your human potentials. They wish you to be a fulfilled human being and seek to do whatever they can to enable this to happen. They can and do act as a connection between you and the rest of humanity. They wish your unique gifts of soul to unfold and integrate well with the needs and unfoldment of humanity, and vice versa.

I call these subtle colleagues our "pit crew." This is purely whimsy on my part, drawn from the image of the NASCAR pit crews that service and support their drivers and their cars during the course of a race. Each of us has a subtle pit crew, a kind of "group Guardian Angel" that seeks to help, if they can, with our incarnation. Whether they *can* help or not depends largely on us and the kind of subtle energy field we generate around ourselves through our thinking, feeling, and behavior. Obviously, if we recognize their existence and seek to come into resonance with their energy, keeping our own subtle field as clear as possible from negative energies or psychic "noise," then our personal "pit crew" can help a great deal, at least to the limit of their capabilities (subtle beings are not all-powerful, after all!). On the other hand, if our personal energy field is murky and dense with thoughts and feelings of fear, hatred, depression, and other negative emotions, it is difficult, though by no means impossible, for them to come close and establish connections.

Although made up of individual beings, it's helpful to think of the Pit Crew as a field of energy, a kind of "incarnational council," that is itself stable throughout our incarnation even though the individuals within it or accessing it may change. As we change and grow, individuals can leave the group and other, newer beings come in as replacements. Yet at the same time, there is a consistency to the "Pit Crew Energy Field" that lasts through the lifetime, anchored in the willingness and intention of its members and participants to serve the incarnational objectives of the soul.

Who makes up a Pit Crew? Here's a diagram of some of the possibilities!

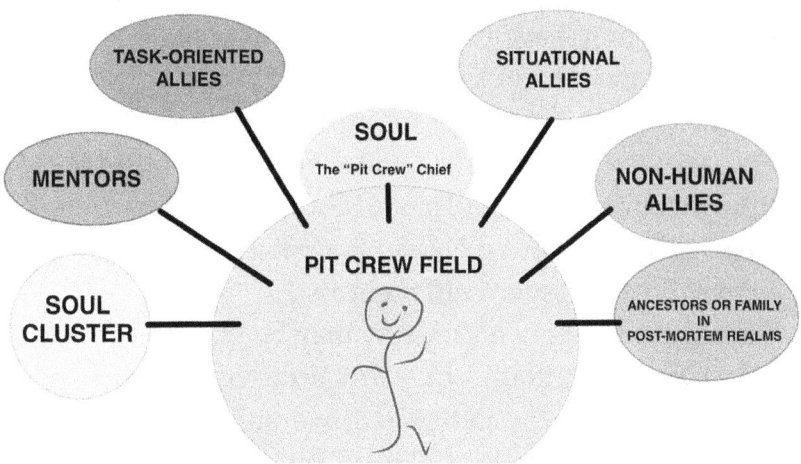

The organizing "heart" and command center of the Pit Crew—the "Crew Chief"—is the Soul of the individual. It establishes the "note" or vibration that determines the overall nature of the incarnation and what the soul hopes to achieve in its physical life. This in turn determines the nature of the Pit Crew Energy Field and thus the kind of subtle beings who may be attracted to or become members of it. Metaphorically, this is like saying the soul determines the kind of car that it's entering into the incarnational race, and this attracts those beings who are familiar with that make and model of racing car and who know how to best service it.

Each of us is part of a soul family which I call a "soul cluster." This is a group of souls who are intimately linked together by similarities of vibration, intentionality, experience, work, and so forth. A deep love pervades such a cluster and unites its members. A soul may be part of more than one soul cluster, just as a person may belong to different groups depending on his or her various interests, but one particular group will be its primary "home" or "family." These are souls who often reincarnate together and have known each other in various roles over many lives; thus, a member of my soul cluster may have been my parent in one life, my child in another, and a lover in yet a third.

A soul may have one or more teachers, guides, or mentors in the subtle realms, more advanced souls who are helping it and others in their soul evolution and journey. An individual's Pit Crew will likely contain a link to one or more beings who act as such soul mentors.

Some members of a Pit Crew may be there because they are task-oriented, that is, they are attracted or connected to a particular work the individual is doing. Some of my Pit Crew, the ones I usually call my subtle colleagues, are like this. We are connected through love, certainly, but mainly through our involvement in the joint project of Incarnational Spirituality. Such subtle colleagues may come and go as the work changes. Unlike members of our soul cluster or the mentors to whom we may be connected, our working allies will usually not stay with us throughout the whole of our lives. Some of my colleagues, for instance, didn't join my Pit Crew until I was in my twenties and had started the work I am doing now. Some of them have since left and others have joined in recent years as the work has evolved.

The same is true for what I call "situational allies." This is a broad category, by which I mean subtle beings who attach to us because of where we are or what is happening around us, i.e., the "situation" in which we are. Such beings come and go and may only be with us for a short period of time in response to some specific condition or environment. For example, during a period of ill health, I might attract someone into my Pit Crew who specializes in healing. Such an ally wouldn't stay once I had regained my health and the crisis was over.

Although our Pit Crew is a connection with the evolving collective spiritual field of Humanity, it may have non-human allies within it. Beings such as nature spirits, elementals, animal spirits, angels, and so on can participate in or contribute to a person's pit crew if the appropriate links and vibrational conditions are present to allow this. For instance, a person dedicated to working with the natural world may well have a nature spirit or an emissary of a nature Deva as part of his or her pit crew. Many people also have "animal powers" or animal spirits working regularly with them, often in shamanic ways. Again, depending on the individual and his or her soul work, they may have one or more angels or Devas as part of their Pit Crew.

It is also possible that individuals who have been part of a person's family or circle of friends in their physical life and who have passed over may remain in touch and become part of that person's Pit Crew, at least for a time. Thus, a father, mother or close friend "on the other side" in the Post-Mortem Realms may choose to remain active in an individual's life and add their energy to the field of the Pit-Crew.

The main criterion is that a member of a person's pit crew knows that person in deep, intimate ways and understands and supports what that soul is seeking to achieve through his or her incarnation. This loving resonance facilitates the energetic connections between the individual and the "pit crew" colleague. It creates a natural alliance. As I said, how a person lives his or her life may obscure or obstruct those connections, but the link of love is always there and can become apparent if the individual changes and makes an effort to "clean up" his or her energy field.

Regrettably, it's possible for an individual whose energy field is dark and filled with negative thoughts and emotions, particularly when these are directed towards others in violent and hurtful ways, to attract a kind of "shadow pit crew" made up of lower-vibrational entities—again, some human, some not—who promote and feed off negative energies. But here the designation "pit crew" is truly inaccurate, for such beings have little or no interest in supporting the individual who has attracted them. Like the parasites they are, they desire only to manipulate and use the person and his or her energies, often against their best interests, in order to generate the negative and hurtful thoughts and emotions on which they thrive. A person's true pit crew is usually a protective force against such dark entities, but they can effectively guard and protect only if the incarnate individual is willing to stop generating and holding the thoughts and feelings that can attract such "bottom-feeders." In all things, we are the responsible parties for the kind of subtle environment we create around ourselves. It is this energetic environment that facilitates or hinders what a person's pit crew can offer.

A person's pit crew isn't a group of beings hovering around that individual 24/7. The individual members of this group have their own lives, their own work, and activities in the subtle realms. However, what they do have is an energetic and perhaps even a telepathic link with the person to whom they are connected, and this permits them to know what is going on and if they are needed. Many subtle beings are multi-tasking in ways that would daunt and overwhelm an incarnate human mind, able to spread their awareness over a great many activities with perfect coordination and harmony. A member of a person's pit crew doesn't need to be "on the scene" or "in the pit stop" all the time, but if there is a need, that being can be there instantly—or as quickly and to the degree that the incarnate individual's energy field permits.

Given the blended nature of individuality in many of

the subtle realms—creating what I call "participatory" or "collaborative" individuality—a subtle Pit Crew ally in his or her natural state may appear to us less like a well-defined person with hard, distinct boundaries and more like a presence whose edges are hard to discern.

Obviously, this isn't the whole picture, as single, distinct individuals can and do appear to incarnates like us, but sometimes in order to do so, they have to draw upon images from our own memories or imaginations. In short, some of their distinct individuality may be co-created by us. I say this not to limit the ability of any subtle being to appear to you and work with you in any way it is able and willing to do so. I say it only to broaden expectations so that you won't miss an ally who appears in one way (as an amorphous presence, for instance, or a cloud of Light) when you are expecting one who appears in a more distinct way. It's work for many subtle beings to project themselves into our vibrational world and into our way of thinking and perceiving. It's like insisting that someone always dress in formal attire every time they come into your presence when all they want to do is to hang out with us in their sweatpants and jerseys.

Here, I am emphasizing the makeup of one's "Pit Crew" as distinct entities, human or otherwise. However, it may be as accurate to describe this as a "Cloud" or "Field" of loving support, a field that is co-generated by the soul and by those beings who aid the incarnation. Using images from quantum physics, this could be described as a "field of potential and possibility," that is, a field that makes possible when needed the manifestation of a helpful ally and presence attuned to the requirements and characteristics of your unique incarnation. This is the main difference between your Pit Crew and another ally you might have. The "Pit Crew Field" is by its very nature attuned to you and is an essential part of your incarnation. This might not be true (at least not initially) with a subtle ally that you invite or encounter in the subtle domains. It's why I consider our Pit Crew a "natural alliance."

Thinking about your Pit Crew as a field of energy may be helpful in that it shifts the emphasis from trying to sense a specific being to sensing an energy field of support and love. Of course, while a being—a "Pit Crew Representative"—can still make himself, herself, or itself known to you, attuning to an energetic field of support may be a good way to start in attuning to this natural alliance. Here is an exercise that suggests one approach to this experience.

Attuning to Your Pit Crew

- Pick a room where you live where you would feel comfortable inviting friends or hosting a party. Sit in that room and take a moment to attune to your Self-Light.

- Look around the room and imagine what its atmosphere or mood would be if you were inviting your closest friends and loved ones—those who care most about you and most wish you to succeed in life—to come into it for a party. Don't imagine anyone in it yet, but just get a felt sense of the kind of hospitable and loving subtle energy you wish the room to have for such a party. Feel that energy within yourself, within your own subtle field, and then expand that out into the room. It's party time!

- When you've filled your room with this energy, imagine what kind of person would be at home within it as a consequence of his or her wishing you the very best. What kind of people would you picture as loving and supporting you? See the room filled with these kinds of people. Welcome them with love and gratitude for their presence.

- What energy have these people brought to your room and your party? Try to have a felt sense of such an energy within yourself. What would you feel like in a room with such people: Safe? Loved? Empowered? Challenged in good ways? Take that feeling into yourself, feel it in your body and in your subtle field, and then expand it out into the room, adding it to the party vibration you created earlier.

- Once you have a sense of this shared field of support and love, lovingly invite someone in this group, that is, in your Pit Crew Energy Field, to step forward and become more distinct and known to you, someone who wishes and is able to connect and interact with you as a subtle partner.

(**Important Note:** If in doing this exercise, you don't experience a specific other presence or an individual being or have difficulty doing so, don't worry. Don't strain to make something happen. There can be various reasons why a being does not make itself known to you in a specific way, whether as the felt sense of a particular presence or as an actual mental or clairvoyant image. Just relax about it and say, "Today, no being!" and let it go. Pay attention to what you *do* feel. Individualities can manifest themselves in different ways which might not fit your expectations, so be open to what is happening.)

- If a being steps forward, ask it what they have to offer? What would they appreciate in return? In other words, what is the nature of the relationship between you? Pay attention to what happens.

- When the encounter seems finished or you are done, thank this being for responding to you. See it step back into the whole Pit Crew Energy Field. Then end the visualization, bringing the "party" to a close, bringing your awareness fully back into your body.

• Let the energy of the experience radiate as a blessing out into your world. Give thanks to your Pit Crew and allies.

• Take a moment to stand in your Sovereignty and ground yourself appropriately. A very good way of grounding is to write about your experience; putting something into words is itself a powerful exercise in connection and grounding. After grounding, go about your daily business.

Transincarnational: Guardian Angel

Each of us has a Guardian Angel. In some ways, it is the spiritual equivalent of our Incarnational Elemental, though the scope of its activity and engagement with our incarnation is broader, encompassing all that aligns us with the Sacred and creates wholeness in our lives. If the Incarnational Elemental is our personal representative from the elemental kingdoms and forces within Gaia, the Guardian Angel is our personal emissary from (and connection with) the angelic kingdom.

Like the Incarnational Elemental, our Guardian Angel is assigned to us to complement our soul's nature and incarnational objectives. As I understand it, like the Incarnational Elemental, the Guardian Angel is with us throughout the entirety of our physical lifetime.

If the soul is our internal, natural participation in sacredness—our inner connection to the Sacred and to the Light—the Guardian Angel is our external connection to the Sacred and to the Light. Like the other "natural allies" though, it is so intimately part of our incarnation that, though it stands separate from us, it is deeply part of us.

The term "guardian" represents one facet of its function in our lives, which is to protect us as best it can within the boundaries that we set, boundaries that are created by the degree of our willingness to listen and respond to the angel's promptings. If we ignore its presence, as many of us do, then that protection can be lessened. It's like a person who has motion detectors around his house to deter burglars but then leaves his windows and doors wide open for anyone to enter.

However, protection is only one function of the Guardian Angel; there are others. It works in whatever way it can (or is allowed by our choices, our karma, and our soul's purposes) to enable us to experience and draw upon our own individual sacredness and to express that sacredness in acts of wholeness in the world. It works in whatever way it can to help us unfold and manifest the full potential of our incarnation, fulfilling the investment of the soul in physical life. It can be a source of healing, guidance, and compassion. It can help us develop the inner poise and silence through which we can better hear the presence and voice of our own soul. It is a servant of the sacredness within us, doing whatever it can, hopefully with our cooperation, to draw the flame of that sacredness into greater and greater Light within us.

To resonate with and attune to one's Guardian Angel is essentially the same process as resonating and attuning to one's soul, as they are both manifestations of a sacred Light.

The Soul

Our soul is without question our number one ally. If we have no other ally, no other subtle partnership in our life, being in communion with our soul is to be in touch with our primary inner teacher, our sacred identity.

But just what exactly is our soul? There are so many different descriptions and definitions of what soul is. We talk about the "soul" of a piece of music or the "soul" of a business; politicians say they are fighting for the "soul of the country." We say something "has soul." We say that someone looks "soulful." We eat "soul food."

In all these cases, we are describing an ineffable inner essence of something, a quality that gives that thing a unique identity, a "flavor of being," a distinct character. This is what our soul is for us, the underpinning and source of our identity and sense of self.

The soul is much more than just this. It is a complex being, only part of which is involved directly in our incarnation. It has other connections, other interactions, other relationships that lie beyond the incarnate world within the ecology of its own level of being.

Here is a diagram I drew that represents my best attempt at describing some of these connections. Think of it as a speculative anatomy of the soul.

A MODEST SPECULATIVE ANATOMY OF THE SOUL

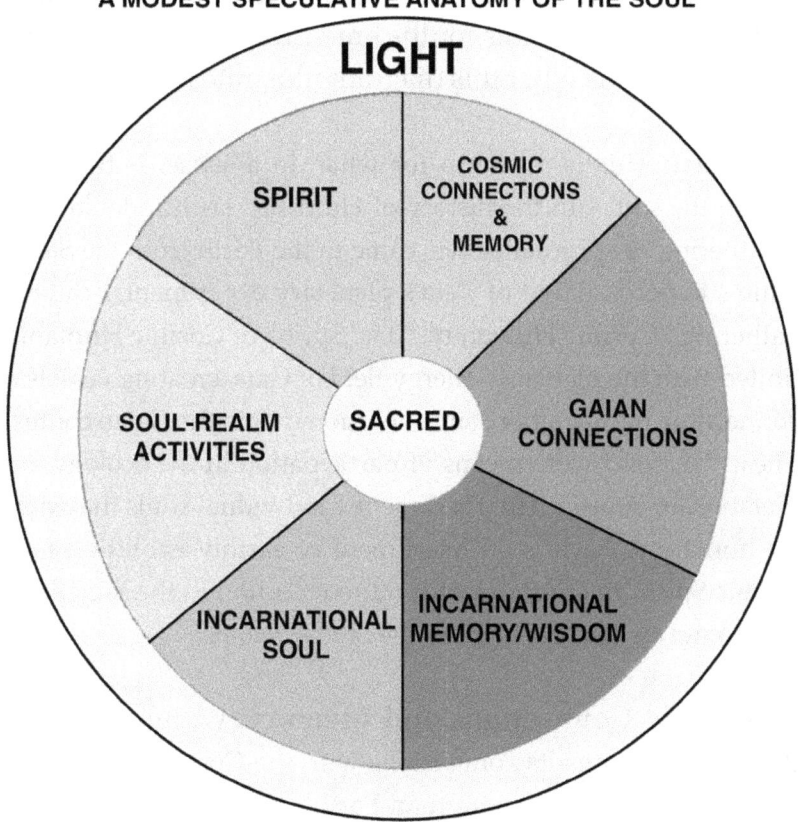

In the first case, the Soul is a Being of Light. Like every other creature, it is an instrument through which the Light of the Sacred manifests itself. When I attune to my soul, my first impression is that of Light. If I have no other experience of my soul or receive nothing else from it that I can discern or understand, the presence of this Light is sufficient. My soul is the source of the sacred Light that enters my life. It is the foundation of that unique emanation that I call my "Self-Light." If I am aware of nothing else about my soul, being able to attune to and draw that Light into my life is wondrous and powerful, healing and renewing.

However, this Light is like a "skin," the radiant emanation

of beingness itself. There is more going on beneath the surface, so to speak, within this multi-dimensional organism that is the soul. That is what this diagram illustrates.

Spirit: This is my term for what, in a sense, is the "soul within the soul." In the history of Humanity as I understand it, a gathering of spiritual beings came to the Earth from the Stellar realms to become part of Gaia's planetary experiment. I call this gathering "Cosmic Humanity." The Spirits of Cosmic Humanity united with the planetary energy field of Gaia, creating vessels of connection, participation, and evolution within the Gaian context. These "vessels" were means of participation in the ecology and metabolism of Gaia. They became the individual souls that make up humanity. Each is an instrument of earthly evolution for a cosmic Spirit. In effect, Spirit is our connection to the sacredness of the cosmos and the Light of the Stellar realms.

Cosmic Connections and Memory: Within the Spirit, the soul maintains its connections with the Cosmos, with those dimensions that are "more-than-Earth" and "more-than-Gaia." Here the soul has access to the memories and wisdom it has accumulated through its cosmic experiences and life. This also represents the connection of the soul to its indwelling Spirit, which is a cosmic entity.

Gaian Connections: As part of the process of Spirit becoming Soul, connections are formed with Gaia and its life. Throughout the history of the soul's evolution and development within the environment of Earth (not just its physical dimension but all its subtle planetary dimensions), these connections expand and deepen so that the soul truly becomes a partner with Gaia and its planetary incarnation. The soul is capable of functioning within as many subtle realms of the world as it has learned to navigate through its connections.

Soul Realm Activities: The soul has its own life and activities as a unique spiritual and sacred identity in relationship with other souls, angels, Devas, and so on. These go on whether a soul is engaged in a physical incarnation or not.

Incarnational Memory and Wisdom: This is the storehouse of the soul's memory of all the physical lives it has lived on the Earth. When we think of remembering past lives, this is the memory we are accessing. Here, too, can be found the wisdom derived from experiences and lessons learned as well as a variety of skills developed through the incarnational process.

Incarnational Soul: This is the aspect of the soul that is currently in incarnation upon the physical earth. Looking "up," so to speak, from the perspective of the personality, we may call this our "High Self." It is that fractal of Soul consciousness, life, and energy that is dedicated to a particular incarnation. It is this incarnational soul that survives bodily death and moves through the various domains of the Post-Mortem worlds, merging on the one hand with its personality counterpart and eventually, on the other hand, with the Soul of which it is a part, moving fully into the wholeness of its soul nature.

Sacred: Of course, this is at the center of it all. Spirit carries the essence of our sacred identity within the soul, and the soul carries our sacred identity into our embodied personalities. Whether we are an incarnate soul manifesting as a human personality or a soul in the subtle worlds or a spirit accessing cosmic dimensions, we are still, always, a sacred identity and presence. This is the core of who we are, however and wherever we are expressing.

Trying to picture a soul's "anatomy" in a two-dimensional fashion is an exercise in futility. The experience of the soul is always much more than any description or definition can fully encompass. It can feel very complex and vast, or it can feel very intimate and simple, such as an embrace of love and Light. You are touching your essential self, or, if you wish, the dynamics out of which "self" emerges. It is more than the personality writ large, but at the same time, it can appear in a very personal way.

However, I hope this diagram gives some sense of the soul as a dynamic focal point of connection and interaction between the sacred, the cosmos, the planetary, and the personal. I hope it conveys a sense that this is what you are, as well.

The most important thing to understand about the soul is that it is neither separated nor distant from our incarnate self. It is part of us, and we are part of it.

This has implications when it comes to attuning to one's soul. There is no one right way to do this as each of us is unique and our relationship to our soul is part of that uniqueness. However, whatever way we use, it's helpful to realize we are not trying to contact something outside of ourselves or distant from us. As the saying goes, our soul is closer to us than our hands or feet.

The key for attuning to any form of life or intelligence is to come into resonance with it. The soul is a being of Light (which, of course, means that fundamentally, we are each beings of Light). How do we resonate with Light? Through our joy, our laughter, our love, our optimism, our patience, our compassion, our fiery hope, our embrace of life, our willingness to create wholeness in ourselves and in our world. How we embody these things in our everyday lives is an ongoing practice of connecting with our soul. We attune to soul by being the qualities of soul.

What complements this practice of soul qualities is listening. I listen all the time, not for words or messages, guidance or counsel but for a sense of inner movement, a flow of energy that carries meaning and direction. As part of this listening, I have found it important to cultivate a sense of inner silence. Silence really is a medium through which the soul speaks. There is so much noise, so many distractions, in the world around us, that we can miss the "still, small voice," that subtle nudge or delicate knowing that is the soul's presence and communication with us. The soul speaks with a voice of love. I have to listen from a place of love as well, loving myself and loving the world.

The Challenge

The Gaian ecology is broken. Put another way, there is disruption within the metabolism of Gaia.

Any ecology is dynamic, always in flux, always in development. The same is true for an organism's metabolism; it is always adapting and adjusting to changes in environment and lifestyle. When I was a young man, I could happily eat anything and not suffer any consequences; I had a cast iron stomach. Now, at 80, this is no longer the case! But I don't feel less healthy now than I did then, only different. My metabolism has changed.

Both ecologies and metabolisms can go through changes, but as long as they remain balanced and the changes don't go to extremes, they can remain healthy. However, certain conditions can disrupt this homeostatic balance—like pollution in an ecosystem or cancer in a body—and push the whole into a crisis state and possibly into collapse and death.

This is where Gaia is today.

We see this manifesting in the climate crisis. We see this

manifesting in the disruptions, stress and violence in the human world. Things are out of balance.

I am aware of two reasons for this, and both involve humanity.

One reason is that in modern society, humanity has deliberately severed itself from communion with the earth as a living presence. It has forgotten or ignored Gaia, which has been necessary in order to treat the world as a dead commodity, a resource to be used for human ends, rather than as a living partner with whom to collaborate in love. We are still part of the Gaia ecosystem, and we are still part of Gaia's energy metabolism, but we have become like a cancer, operating independently from the larger whole and creating obstruction to the healthy flow of vital subtle energies. The current understanding of "business as usual" is killing us and killing the world (or at least the world with which we are familiar, and which has been unusually hospitable to us).

This condition is exacerbated by the weight of millennia of unresolved and unhealed thought-forms and habits created by human activity, thought, and feeling which perpetuate hatreds, rivalries, fears, and modes of thinking that are divisive and often malignant. This psychic karma and residue of trauma work against human wholeness at both individual and collective levels, creating further disruption of the healthy flow of vital subtle and spiritual energies within the body of Gaia.

The second reason is that Gaia itself is undergoing a change, what esoterically we might consider a "cosmic initiation." I am aware of vast, new spiritual energies and qualities becoming part of the overall life and beingness of Gaia, coming from spiritual sources beyond this world. The entirety of Gaia's ecosystem is needing to adapt to these new energies and possibilities. Its whole organic metabolism is needing to adapt and integrate this new stimulus.

(If you want a pop culture metaphor for what is happening, think of the Marvel movie *Captain America* in which a skinny, weak, undernourished Steve Rogers is given a Super Soldier serum that turns him into super strong, well-muscled, dynamic Captain America. In a sense, we are part of the emergence of Captain Gaia as a serum of Cosmic Spirit begins to take hold!)

This change is stimulating and affecting all parts of Gaia, some of which are easily adapting and some of which need help—or cannot adapt at all and thus are phased out. The challenge is with humanity. Many humans are feeling these deep inner changes, and their souls are responding and adapting, though often not without struggle at the outer personality level. Other people are afraid of what is happening—fear often comes with change—and are resisting these new energies or are unable to adapt to them in their current incarnation. This only adds to the disruption and stress within the collective energy field of humanity. It's as if, in the *Captain America* movie, many of Steve Roger's cells resisted and fought against the effects of the serum. Pain is the result.

A new "Gaian Human" is struggling to emerge in response to the changes and potentials now active within Gaia's ecology. But it can seem like trying to pull oneself free from the sucking undertow of quicksand built from habit and misalignment with the whole.

The Response

I am aware of the spiritual worlds responding to this challenge. It's a complex response—after all, Gaia is a complex organism—but a simple way to think of it is that vast resources of Light are being created that can assist in the reception, adaptation to, and integration of these new spiritual energies (as if a second serum has been created to help Steve Roger's body receive and adapt to the Super Soldier Serum).

If humanity is a major part of what is challenging the health and wholeness of Gaia, it is also an important part of what will meet this challenge, bringing healing and new potentials to the fore. The reason is that we have the soul capacity—and the Incarnational capacity—to partner with the higher realms of Light where these resources are assembled and to be collaborative conduits for these new energies to become an integrated part of the world.

This is a spiritual work. It is a subtle energy work. It is a call to a partnership with spirit. As such, it draws on all our resources, physical, subtle, and spiritual, to do this work successfully. Our ability to bring loving energies into our subtle environment through our blessing partnership is essential as a foundation for this calling. Equally, having the support of our natural allies, our Entelechy, gives us a subtle energy structure that can more easily and gracefully align with, hold, and integrate the incoming Light of the higher dimensions.

PART IV: FOUNDATIONAL THOUGHTS

Perception: Beyond Seeing and Hearing

I think of perception as a relationship between four elements, each of which contributes to its particular piece. These four elements are the environment that provides the stimuli; the sensory organ or methodology that receives these stimuli and converts them into information; the brain or organizing instrument that collects, processes and compiles this information; and the mind that interprets that compilation and determines what has been perceived.

For instance, we have a variety of birds that live in the trees around our house and visit our bird feeders on the back porch. My wife, Julie, will remark about how beautiful their bird song is. In this case, the birds are singing, creating sound waves in the environment which Julie's ears receive and translate into bioelectrical impulses that travel to the brain. There, these signals are transformed into a perception that Julie then interprets as "bird song" or "music."

In my own case, though, this doesn't happen. The birds can be singing and the sound waves impacting my ears, and my ears can be converting the pressure of these sound waves into bioelectric impulses, but there it stops. A bad case of measles when I was six years old left me partly deaf. There's nothing wrong with the actual structure of the ear but many of the nerves that receive and process the bioelectric signals from the ear are dead. There are frequencies of sound that I do not and cannot hear. My brain has lost the ability to process them.

The result of this dysfunction in my brain is that I do not hear most bird songs. Julie can be rhapsodizing over how lovely the birds sound, but all I hear is silence, or if I do hear something at the edge of my range, it doesn't sound like music, only like noise. In fact, as far as I'm concerned, if I didn't see the birds, I would not know they were there, and if I were skeptically inclined, I could accuse Julie of making it all up. I could tell her that bird song is just something "in her head," a figment of her imagination.

Which, of course, is what many skeptics say about people like myself who experience subtle perceptions.

From my perspective, everyone has the innate ability to receive information and impulses from the non-physical world; we are doing it all the time, just as my ears are always feeling the pressure of the sound waves caused by birds' singing and other high-pitched frequencies of sound. What most people lack is a way of processing and interpreting this information. My inability to hear birds is a function of actual damage to certain nerves in my brain, but the inability of most people to be aware of subtle perceptions is due more to inactivity and inattention so that the brain areas that link to such perceptions are not developed. This is not entirely a physical issue, either, for attitudes and beliefs play a role here. Our mental and emotional states affect what we perceive, and in the case of subtle perception, an unwillingness to accept the possibility of such an awareness or to trust it when it happens can diminish or obstruct its development.

Part of the challenge in developing and using subtle perception lies in not knowing how to think about it. Our attitudes and expectations, even when we're willing to believe in the possibility of such perception, can affect how smoothly such development can occur.

Here's an example of what I mean. When I'm working with a group discussing subtle perception, invariably someone will say, "Oh, I don't see anything," or "I don't hear anything." There is often a sense of finality about this as if the lack of seeing and hearing closes the door to any kind of awareness of a non-physical reality. But the purpose of a sensory function is to convey information about the environment in which one is embedded so that one may connect and engage with it. Eyes and ears do it one way, but they aren't the only ways that are possible. Consider that in the subtle dimensions, there are no photons of light to excite optic nerves with vision or sound waves to exert pressure upon ear drums to produce the phenomenon of sound. These are physical phenomena, and our physical senses are developed and adapted to them. But if I expect that all sensory information is going to come to me in a manner akin to my physical senses, then I will be less able to recognize such information when it comes in a fashion dictated by the requirements of its own unique environment.

The subtle worlds are environments of energy and thought. There are modes of perception that are adapted to such environments, and they convey that information to our minds in ways that have nothing to do with sight or sound. So, the first thing I need to understand in developing subtle perception is that I don't have to "see" or "hear" anything in order to perceive into the subtle worlds. I can apprehend what is present around me in other ways. I know from my own experience that it's possible to train the brain to be receptive to energy modes of perception but to do so, I need to mindfully resist the habit of wanting my sensory information to come in familiar packages. I have to go beyond seeing or hearing into other forms of sensitivity.

And yet, there is no doubt that people do "see" and "hear" in the subtle realms. In some cases, this may actually be due to subtle organs of sense that mimic these functions, such as the legendary "third eye" of clairvoyance. But in most cases, it's due to the interpretive function of perception. I don't have to have light waves hitting my eyes to see something. Subtle energies and impulses of thought can trigger visual responses within the mind, resulting in an inner sight. In fact, this is precisely the use of the imagination as an organ of perception.

We experience this when we read a novel filled with rich descriptions. Visually we are only seeing word symbols on a page, but imaginatively, whole worlds arise before our inner eyes, allowing us to see and hear what the author wants us to see and hear. We are taking information in from our environment (the book) to create information in our minds. In the process, we can see and hear what isn't there in a physical sense.

Still, if I can free myself of a dependence on using sight and sound as my primary models for sensory perception and thus from expectations built around those models, I will be in a better position to appreciate and learn subtle awareness as a unique experience in its own right and not simply as physical perception in non-physical guise.

Modes of Perception

In the physical world, we have nine senses which medical science divides into two categories, special and somatic. The special senses are so-called because they rely on special organs; they include sight, hearing, taste, and smell. The somatic senses, on the other hand, are diffused throughout the whole body. The body itself is the organ that perceives, rather than some specialized part of it. These senses include touch, the sensitivity to pressure and vibration; thermoception, the sensitivity to temperature and heat; nociception, the sensitivity to pain; and proprioception, the sensitivity to the body's position and movement in space. A ninth sense is balance, a vestibular sense which some sources think of as a special sense because it functions through the inner ear and others classify as a somatic sense because it is felt throughout the body.

We don't think much about the somatic senses, other than touch, precisely because they are not focused in such a specific way as sight and hearing. The information the somatic senses convey forms the background of my life for the most part. Yet, it's been my experience that the further one moves in consciousness into the Subtle Worlds, the nature of sensory experience becomes more and more "somatic," involving the whole of one's subtle energy field and less and less focused around a specific perceptual organ. This is why in developing subtle perception, it's important to free ourselves of expecting to "see" and "hear" in the way we do physically. It may happen, but more likely, it will not. Subtle perception is more like "feeling" than like "seeing."

In fact, as one moves progressively through the subtle and spiritual worlds, the senses begin to blend into a form of perception that merges sight, sound, touch, smell, taste, and even knowing or cognition into a single, unified percept. For this reason, when I talk about "feeling" as a subtle somatic sense, I'm really talking about an awareness that delivers much more information than does physical touch.

There is a lake about half a mile from my house. If I stand on the lakeshore, I see the lake. But if I step into it, I not only see it, but I am immersed in it. My eyes still see the lake as something apart from me, but my body feels the lake's presence all over me, surrounding me, and my somatic senses tell me I'm floating in the water. I now feel something my eyes could not tell me; I feel the phenomenon of being wet.

This kind of immersive and expansive experience is very much part of what subtle senses convey to me. They don't just give me information; they connect me to the world around me. I don't just *see*; I become *part of*. I think of this as *participatory perception*.

Special senses tend to give me a sense of being an observer. The somatic senses, however, give me a feeling of participation. I don't observe my balance as something outside of me, for example. Balance is something I participate in. Subtle senses, as they become increasingly "somatic" in their expression, also convey more and more of a sense of participation. I don't just observe; I become one with. The information which these subtle senses convey comes out of this sense of oneness, of being immersed in and blended with that which I perceive.

I illustrate the different modes of perception in the following picture:

MODES OF PERCEPTION

PHYSICAL WORLD	SUBTLE WORLDS	SPIRITUAL REALMS
SOMATIC SENSES TOUCH (Pressure, Vibration) THERMOCEPTION (Temperature) NOCICEPTION (Pain) PROPRIOCEPTION (Position) BALANCE (Vestibular)	SUBTLE KINESTHESIA (Energy Touch) CLAIRSENTENCE EMPATHY FIELD SENSITIVITY (Atmospheres, Moods)	"HOLOCEPTION" (Perception through Blending, Oneness, Presence, & Identity) "Participatory Perception"
SPECIAL SENSES SIGHT HEARING TASTE SMELL	CLAIRVOYANCE CLAIRAUDIENCE TELEPATHY	

THE PERCEPTUAL FIELD

Over the years, I've come to appreciate that we each inhabit a perceptual field which in itself is unlimited in its scope, potentially connecting to a universe of information. How much of that field we can actually access and how much of what we access we can actually interpret and understand, is another matter. As incarnate beings, we access this perceptual field through our physical senses. Our subtle nature accesses this field in different ways, giving us different—often more expanded and inclusive—kinds of information about the world around us.

My experience is that as one moves in consciousness through different subtle frequencies and into the spiritual worlds, the sensory experience becomes more "somatic" than "special" in its nature; our whole being increasingly becomes the sensory organ rather than depending on specific organs such as eyes or ears.

The subtle equivalent to the somatic senses may include such phenomena as subtle kinesthesia or energy awareness, empathy, clairsentience (a sense of intuitive knowing), and "field perception" (which is a perception of subtle "atmospheres" through one's subtle field). In the spiritual realms, this somatic form of perception increases, becoming something I call *holoception*, or perception through one's whole being. This conveys a deep, soulful kind of knowledge that is as much communion as communication or perception. The nature of a being unfolds itself like a flower opening its petals, and I experience this (or as much of it as I'm able) not as something happening outside myself but as something in which I am participating. So, for instance, I may perceive a nature spirit and that perception may include knowing what it is, what it's doing, and its relationship to a particular tree or shrub or plot of ground. I see its connections and experience them as my connections. It's as if in that moment, I become the nature spirit.

This picture is not intended as a complete description of all possible forms of subtle perception. It's just a "visual field note" of my own experiences. Your experience might be different, so you should feel free to expand this chart, or for that matter, ignore it. You certainly should not feel constrained by it in any way.

But here is a final speculative thought. It may well be that in fact there is really only one sense, a "master" or "universal" sensory function whose ultimate purpose is to enable participation and connection within an environment. What we experience as our nine physical senses may then simply be refractions of this master sense in the same way that the colors of a rainbow are all refractions of white light. As we move away from the physical plane, our sensory capacities begin to blend and unify as we gain greater capacity to engage with the larger perceptual field and the "master sense" which it represents. As we do so, it becomes harder and harder—and less meaningful—to talk about specific subtle senses in the way we talk about (and experience) our physical senses. There cease to be specific senses, but only one sense, a "holoception" in which wholeness reaches out to wholeness in mutual participation and oneness.

Perception as Participation

When my wife, Julia, hears bird song, it brings her joy, and she has a sense of being part of nature. In effect, she is changed in that she becomes more than just an isolated person with her personal senses; she becomes part of a greater whole, one shared by all life. Perception becomes participation. This is a "holoception" we can all take part in.

Perception is a relationship, not between separate parts but between participants united in an emerging wholeness. I don't hear bird song, but I can see birds. We have crows that come and sit on the railing of our back porch. Sometimes, when Julie and I are just sitting on the porch together, reading or just quietly soaking in the sunlight, one of the crows will come and sit with us, its legs folded under it, also soaking up the sunshine and cleaning its ebony feathers, keeping us company. There's a sense of friendship between us.

The crows that visit us are in no way "pets;" they are wild birds, but still, we share a companionable relationship, each of us giving the other space just to be who we are. We see each other, and in a wonderful way, seeing myself through the crow's eyes takes me beyond my humanness into a Gaian realm shared by all of us.

When we perceive the world, we become the world. Our habits and attitudes can blind us to this and convince us we are separate. Then we may carry that sense of separateness over into our perceptions, dealings, and partnerships with the subtle worlds. When this happens, when we insist on "seeing" and "hearing" or sensing as separate beings, we diminish the possibilities of participation in the wholeness of Gaia's full ecology. Ironically, therefore, our first steps into partnership with spirit lie with learning how to partner in attentive and loving ways with the physical world that surrounds us. Partnership with spirit is participation with spirit, which in the wholeness of things, also means participation with the world in which we live.

More Than Psychology

When I am served a slice of moist chocolate cake, there is a physical component to that experience—the sight, the smell, the taste of that cake—but there is also a psychological component. I may feel delighted. I may feel anxious ("How many calories does this have?"). I may be thinking about cakes I've had in the past ("This doesn't look like the cake Mom used to bake!"). I may be repelled because (poor me!) I'm allergic to chocolate. Eating it, I may experience joy, ecstasy, pleasure, or if the baker accidentally used salt instead of sugar in the recipe, horror and disgust.

The point is that we almost immediately and automatically translate a physical experience into a psychological one. We evaluate what we're experiencing. This usually does not affect the physical environment or the object itself. The fact that I'd prefer a lemon cake doesn't alter the presence of chocolate in the slice of chocolate cake; that I don't like plunging into cold water doesn't change the temperature of the water. My discomfort doesn't make the water colder or hotter. However, eating something I don't like can cause indigestion, a physical response to an emotional reaction. My father suffered from digestive problems as he got older, but when he ate out at a restaurant he loved, it didn't matter what he ate, he never had stomach problems afterward. His joy at the experience shifted his body chemistry, at least for that meal!

The same thing happens with subtle energy experiences. The big difference is that subtle energies, particularly those whose frequency is "close to" or less different from the physical world, are thought-sensitive and responsive to our thinking and feeling. This means that our reaction to contact with a subtle presence can affect the nature of that contact. If we are fearful, for instance, our fear can turn an otherwise loving contact into something frightening, causing the potential subtle ally to withdraw so as not to cause harm or distress. In the subtle worlds, it's possible that my desire for a lemon cake would transform the chocolate flavor into lemon.

This is one reason that training to work with subtle partners almost always involves establishing a center of calmness in which psychological responses are stilled to perceive more clearly exactly what kind of energy presence we're contacting and to avoid unwanted reactions that can alter the nature of the experience.

When it comes to discernment, our physical and psychological responses can be important clues to the kind of subtle presence that is seeking to engage with us. We don't want to become so neutral and numb that we have no response at all. But there is a balance here, and it can take some practice to learn. It's the balance between being still enough to have accurate insight into the energies accompanying a subtle contact and being open to signals of warning, usually coming from our own subtle field and impacting our body, our thoughts, and our feelings in some manner. The energy of some subtle beings can be different enough from what we're used to, or it can be so intense that it registers alarm and a desire to pull away, even though the intent from the subtle side is benign with no desire to harm or frighten. Handling such a challenging contact with grace and calm so that it has a chance to reveal its true nature requires understanding our own psychology and having control over our reactions. Metaphorically, it's stilling our desire for lemon flavor so that the chocolate in the cake can present itself as chocolate.

The second point when dealing with subtle energy phenomena is to avoid psychologizing them. You want to avoid reducing subtle and spiritual experiences into purely psychological experiences, interpreting and thus reducing objective subtle energy phenomena into subjective psychological constructs. These are two different domains, but because we are so familiar with the psychological perspective on the world and less familiar with a subtle energy perspective, we tend to collapse the two together as if they were the same, not respecting the differences.

This means being careful when we use psychological terms to describe subtle phenomena or experiences. Such terms can seem to offer an attractive alternative to using physical analogies or metaphors. Because we may understand what the psychological description means, we might jump to a conclusion about what the subtle phenomenon means. Because subtle energies can produce subjective psychological effects, using psychological terms to identify those effects can give us the illusion of understanding the actual subtle phenomenon that caused those effects. The risk is that of turning the objective reality of the subtle worlds into personal subjective states.

Here is a very basic example. Take the word *love*. We all know what it means psychologically as an emotion. We use terms like affection, caring, attraction, and so on to describe it. But when I talk about love as a subtle force, I don't mean any of those things. Love, energetically, is not an emotion but a force, like gravity in the physical world but even more fundamental. It is the force or presence that enables the created universe to behave as a coherent whole that allows for sacredness, the generative source of life and being, to emerge and manifest itself. Love is a force creating wholeness. In doing so, it can repel as much as attract; it can manifest as separation as much as togetherness if that separation serves the emergence of a more vital and dynamic wholeness. Love could keep things apart that, if they were to come together, would be mutually annihilating or at least disruptive.

The issue of not psychologizing subtle energy experiences and turning them into purely personal subjective experiences is a fundamental challenge based on habits of thinking. In hundreds of classes over the years, I discovered that one of the biggest problems people can have in experiencing the subtle realms is the tendency to explain everything psychologically and to look for a psychological reason for what they are experiencing. There may be such a reason—as I said above, subtle phenomena can create psychological responses as much as, if not more than, physical phenomena do—but it will be only part of the picture. If a person is satisfied with that psychological explanation and stops there, he or she will fail to perceive a deeper level of meaning and contact with an objective non-physical reality that provides the subtle part of the experience.

In other words, the subtle and spiritual realms are objective realities, not subjective images or projections. They need to be respected and treated as such.

Learning to deal with subtle phenomena as their own reality means living in our subtle energy nature as much as we do in our minds and in our bodies. There is very little in our modern culture and society that supports this. Mostly what it takes is attention, willingness, and practice. It is not a question of being psychic or highly developed spiritually, nor is it the result of a specific technique, though there are techniques and practices that can help. Living "energetically" as well as physically and psychologically is a natural part of who we are. It is built into us. It is part of our wholeness. We simply need to recover the skill at doing so. We need to remember who we are.

One excellent way to do this is through the blessing partnership we discussed earlier. This is both a way to bring positive energies into one's environment and a way to practice thinking and acting as a person who is part of a subtle energy world as well as a physical one.

Another excellent exercise is to make a daily practice of attuning to one or more of your natural allies or to the subtle sense of your Entelechy as a whole. These are the subtle beings closest to you, even part of you, and thus the easiest with whom to practice your subtle energy awareness.

Imagination and Anthropomorphizing

In my experience, one of the biggest challenges people face in learning how to form alliances and partnerships with subtle beings lies in the words, "It's just my imagination." We are so accustomed in our Western culture to seeing the imagination as an instrument of fantasy that it can be hard to also see it as an organ of perception. So often when we speak of something as "imaginary," we understand it to be unreal.

Ultimately, all perception ends up as imagination. Information in the form of electromagnetic energy, pressure, temperature, or sound waves interacts with our senses which translate it into biochemical and bioelectrical impulses in the brain, which in turn form a corresponding picture of the world. This picture is imaginary, a product of the brain's ability to form sensory imagery. Further, research has proven that this inner world is different for each person because our individual nervous systems and brains are different. We are all neurodivergent. This difference is usually slight enough that we are able to construct a shared perception of the world, a common reality we all agree on, but this is not always the case. As I mentioned, there are sounds that simply do not exist in my world but do in my wife's, and likely in yours. The same is true for odor as I was born with a very reduced sense of smell. People often exclaim over the smell of something cooking or the aroma of coffee (or flowers, for that matter), but I have to take their word for it. I smell nothing. In my world, flowers do not have fragrances.

However, I was born with a sensitivity to subtle energies. I believe most of us are, but circumstances, training, and family pressures suppress it. In my case, this most often took the form of a subtle kinesthesia in which I could feel the play of subtle energies against my own subtle body and its "skin," a field that extends some feet outside my physical body. Just as with physical sensations, this subtle touch conveyed information that my brain interpreted in various ways, often but not always visually. My perceptual field takes in information from more than just the physical world, but it is still processed and interpreted the same way in my brain, largely using the faculty of imagination or the ability to create images.

It's confusing to have one word that applies to two different functions; the function of perception, and the function of creative fantasy, the faculty that allows us to perceive possibilities that do not yet exist, to compose music, to paint great art, or to tell wonderful stories.

As a result, when people have a subtle sensory experience, perceiving something that is outside the range of their physical senses, they dismiss it as "just my imagination." This is a habit that is hard to break, especially because fantasy does exist. Not everything we imagine *is* real, and both our physical and subtle senses can deceive us (or more precisely, the brain erroneously interprets what the senses are conveying). When I'm telling a story, I'm likely creating a world that doesn't exist, even though I may see it clearly in my mind's eye. To say that the story world is objectively real in the way my living room is real, or the city of Seattle is real, is to court delusion.

We live in a world of concrete shapes and patterns, a world of definite imagery. Subtle beings do not. How much they do not depends on what they are and their native place, their *noöregion,* within the ecology of the subtle and spiritual worlds. Often, in order to connect and communicate with us, they reach into our imaginations to give themselves forms with which we can relate, usually a human appearance. For example, my visual impression of my subtle colleague, John, was that of a sphere of coruscating Light, but when he first appeared to me, he did so in the form of a stereotypical college professor, tweed jacket and all. This was a form he knew I could relate to. Similarly, I have had contact with angels that look like radiant humans, but usually when I see angels, they appear as multi-colored, dynamic and shifting geometric forms, like something I might see in a kaleidoscope. This is partly because a being like John or like angels, exist in more than three dimensions but my brain doesn't know how to interpret such multidimensionality. This evolved to deal with a world of three dimensions.

A friend of mine who is an accomplished seer, someone well-experienced in dealing with the subtle worlds and subtle beings, once was in conversation with a being who had the appearance of a radiant and beautiful human being. He asked it to show him what it really looked like when it wasn't projecting a human shape, probably using his imaginative faculty to do so. The being refused, saying that it could hurt him, and that it didn't wish to cause any harm. However, my friend persisted until finally, the being agreed to reveal part of its true self. It did so, and my friend said he recoiled in pain, not because he saw something horrible or frightening but because his mind couldn't interpret and understand what he *was* seeing. Its multi-dimensionality was so far outside his realm of comprehension that his mind couldn't encompass it, and it hurt mentally to do so.

It's no wonder that angels are often described as having multiple wings and eyes all over their bodies! It's an attempt to capture the sense of a being whose natural shape is much more than three-dimensional.

Over the years I've grown used to the fact that subtle and spiritual beings in their native state usually look nothing like anything I might see in the physical world around me; they are, after all, beings of Light and energy. But when starting out, it was useful that they appeared in familiar forms, often drawn from my imagination or from the mythic images of human culture. Had I said, "Oh, this is just my imagination at play," it would have short-circuited the contact and the communication. No collaborative mind or field would have been possible.

Imagination plays a critical role in contacting and communicating with subtle and spiritual beings. It's a powerful tool, one we need to respect but also one we need not discard. To say that something is "only my imagination" need not be the end but just the first step towards apprehending, appreciating, and understanding just what is in contact with us.

With this in mind, I want to say something about anthropomorphizing, imaginatively giving something human characteristics and personality. I've had students say that they are concerned that they are anthropomorphizing their inner contact, giving it a human shape and demeanor. This may indeed be true, but as I said above, there can be a reason for this, as it's easier to comprehend and communicate with something that looks and acts like us than with something that is totally outside our range of physical experience. Subtle and spiritual beings can and do appear in human forms to facilitate contact, at least in the beginning.

Still, care must be taken not to confuse the image—which may be a tool of communication—with the reality, that is, with that which is communicating. There's nothing inherently wrong with anthropomorphizing as long as you are aware that this is going on and that it may be only a layer of convenience. I know from experience that it can be easier to talk with something that looks like a person than with something that is a cloud of Light or simply a quality like Peace or Love.

We do give personalities to the inanimate things that we work with. We talk about our cars or houses or favorite furniture as if they were alive. The thing is, on a subtle level, they are. As I describe in my book, *Techno-Elementals*, they contain living energies. It's quite possible to project human personalities onto these things, to anthropomorphize them, as a beginning step to more deeply exploring just what these living energies are. If I think of my couch as a living person, it opens up a new and deeper level of engagement and relationship with it than if I just think of it as an artifact, a piece of furniture. This, in turn, can lead me to an inner attunement with that subtle life itself and its unique characteristics, but

I will need to let go of my anthropomorphic projections to do so. They can be a convenient and fun step into the rich life of the subtle and spiritual worlds, but it's important to remember that, with few exceptions, these are not human worlds. We are encountering beings and forces with their own sacred nature and characteristics, which we need to honor and respect.

Saying No!

In all dealings with subtle or spiritual beings—or with subtle energies in general—you have the absolute right to say NO! to anything you are asked to believe or do. When my subtle colleague and mentor, John, first came to me in 1965, one of the first things he said was this: "Always feel free to say no to me. If you don't feel you can say no, then you're not truly free to say yes."

The point John wished to make is that he did not want obedience from me; he wanted collaboration and partnership. He did not want me to see him as my superior; he wanted me to see him as an equal, meaning that in our relationship, we were co-creative equals. We might be very different in our energy fields—John was certainly a more powerful being energetically than I was—but we are equal in our sacredness.

Part of this equality is the right to respect your own boundaries, values, and freedom and the right to say "No!" should you feel any of these are being violated or trespassed upon in some manner. No matter who a subtle being says or claims he or she is, that being is never closer to God than you are. We are all equally sacred, even if very different energetically. That equality gives you the right to say NO.

You can certainly say NO if you disagree with something a subtle being is presenting to you or asking you to do. But sometimes the NO needs to arise not out of disagreement but out of a temporary mismatch between your subtle energy field and that of the subtle contact. It is not at all unusual for a subtle being to misjudge how much subtle energy an incarnate human can absorb or integrate in the moment. It can feel as if someone has stepped right up against you, invading your personal space, while trying to say something. If it were a physical person doing that, you would ask them to step back. You can do the same with a subtle or spiritual contact, letting them know that their energy is overwhelming you or is more than you can handle in that moment. This is a modified NO, but a NO nonetheless, letting your contact know you need more space.

Whatever the reason, just know that you can always say NO to the subtle realms. It's best if this NO arises out of honoring your own boundaries, values, and freedom, and does not come out of fear. It is more powerful if it arises from your strength and your sense of your own Sovereignty.

It's the Incarnation

In the final analysis, in working with subtle forces or beings, it's important to remember that you are an incarnate person whose soul has chosen to be part of the physical world. The wholeness and integrity of your incarnate life are important. If contact with the subtle ecologies of Gaia threatens this or brings imbalance into your life, then it is time to back away from such contacts until they can be integrated into the wholeness of your incarnation.

When I began working with John, my first subtle mentor, he insisted that I have one or more hobbies, things that I loved doing just as a person and that had nothing to do with spirituality or with working with subtle beings. He wanted me to have a well-rounded personal life that would balance the work I was doing with him or with other subtle beings.

What brought me joy as a person? What did I do just for fun? What did I do that honored me as a personality as well as the things I did that honored me as a soul?

The point is to honor each of the Gaian ecosystems of which we are a part or to which we are attuned. For me, the subtle environment and the subtle and spiritual worlds are environments of which I am aware and with which I have dealings. I live part of my life in them. But I am also part of the physical world, the world of my body, the world of my mind and feelings, and I need to honor them as well. Our challenge is to be whole beings, Gaian humans who are at home within the whole planetary ecology—the whole metabolism and organism—of Gaia, but we cannot achieve this if we neglect or diminish the wholeness of our physical and psychological incarnate life.

We need to be wholly here if we are to be wholly everywhere.

PART V: THE GAIAN HUMAN

The Stellar Earth

This book is about forming partnerships and collaborative alliances with subtle and spiritual beings. Not just any kind of partnership, however, but those of a particular kind; partnerships designed to serve Gaia, the planetary soul, and Humanity at a time of need and change. In the previous chapters, I described the earth as a living organism whose metabolism is made up of flows and exchanges of spirit and energy, mediated by spiritual, subtle, and physical beings (including ourselves). This metabolism is changing. All beings within the ecology of Gaia's life are needing to change and adapt as well. Lines and flows of energy that have been blocked need to be opened up; new connections and flows need to be discovered and established.

When we think of Gaia, we think of the *anima mundi*, the soul of the world, but we may forget that we are also talking about a star of life existing in its own cosmic environment. It's much the same way that as children, we know our parents as Mom and Dad, special presences within the family and sources of love and nourishment, but we don't know the larger life and environment in which they live outside the family.

When I was six years old, I was happily living in a house in Palo Alto, California, not far from Stanford University. Then, all at once, we were moving, not just to another neighborhood or city but to another country, Morocco. Seemingly out of the blue, my loving mother, who was a Registered Nurse working in a hospital, was giving me painful injections to inoculate me against a variety of African diseases. Why? I only knew from what Mom said that Dad's work was taking him to Morocco, and we were going with him. I knew nothing about the Korean War taking place at the time, or the Cold War with Russia, or that Dad was an intelligence agent working for the U.S. Military who had been assigned to do counter-intelligence work against Soviet agents working in Morocco. I only knew that change was upon me. Forces and circumstances outside my experience and knowledge had intervened, and nothing would be the same.

Something similar is happening to Gaia, and as a result, change is upon us. What do we know, what can we know, of the reasons for this or of the nature of the forces instigating this change? They are part of a multidimensional cosmic environment—Gaia's cosmic environment—about which we know little and can probably understand even less.

I became aware of these changes many years ago when I was a teenager but only in the most general way, like looking up in the sky, seeing clouds in the distance, and knowing that rain is on its way. Later, when I began working with my first subtle colleague and mentor, a non-physical individual I named "John," I began to gain, with his help, a deeper understanding of what was happening. It was this knowledge that led to my involvement with what became the New Age Movement. Still, even to this day, I probably know as much about the deeper processes at work at cosmic levels as I knew as a child of six about why we were moving to Morocco!

What I do understand, I tell as a story. Gaia is part of its own cosmic environment. Although we might think of this environment as being our solar system and interstellar space beyond, that is only its physical expression. Beyond this, extending into multidimensional realms lies what I call the "stellar realm." Part of this realm is associated with the stars and planets we see in the night sky, but much if not most of it is not, at least not directly (in the cosmos, as with Gaia, everything is ultimately interconnected). I think of it as the spiritual realm from which galaxies and stars emerge as physical manifestations of metaphysical processes and relationships.

Gaia is part of this stellar realm. Gaia is, in effect, a star, but one whose physical expression is that of a planet rather than a sun; a planet so conducive to and filled with life that it becomes a "star of life," radiating the qualities and powers of life into the universe.

Within this stellar environment, Gaia grows and has relationships just as we do in our own environments. There are stellar beings who are particularly involved with and supportive of Gaia's planetary incarnation just as there are subtle and spiritual beings—our "Natural Alliances"—who do the same with us.

The stellar realm is dynamic; nothing is static, staying the same. New energies, new possibilities, new challenges, and new relationships become available, just as they do for us in our incarnations. This is exactly what is happening for Gaia. It is encountering a "stepping up," an intensification or a broadening of spiritual energies available to it.

This is happening, as I understand it, both as a result of changes in Gaia's cosmic environment, as our planet seems to be entering an area of heightened spiritual energy, and as a result of specific interventions and gifts of energy coming from certain of Gaia's stellar mentors and "natural allies." These latter are by way of assisting Gaia to adapt to and make the best use of the influx of cosmic energies now available to the world soul.

Whatever the source of these new energies, the overall effect is a pressure to change upon the internal metabolism and ecosystem of Gaia as new capabilities become available.

Over the years, I've thought of various metaphors to try to explain this. In an occult or esoteric context, I could say that Gaia is undergoing a cosmic initiation, taking on and needing to integrate a new and higher frequency or potency of spiritual energy than it has embodied before. Or, using an entirely different metaphor, I could say that Gaia is like a member of a barbershop quartet that has now expanded to become part of a large choir that is tackling more complex musical pieces. As such, Gaia is learning new harmonies and new arrangements and needing to blend with many more voices. Or we could imagine the physiological and metabolic changes that occur in our bodies when we go through puberty.

Earlier, I used a metaphor from the popular superhero genre. In the movie, *Captain America* the Marvel superhero, short, scrawny, weak Steve Rogers is given a Super Soldier serum that transforms him into tall, muscled, super strong Captain America. It seems to me something similar is happening with Gaia. The introduction of new energies of spirit and life is stimulating change, making our planetary soul stronger in its connections and relationships with its cosmic environment. Hello to Captain Gaia!

I do not know all the effects of this. Here in the incarnate physical realm, we may never see all the effects, or they may take centuries, even millennia, to manifest. But there are two consequences that I am aware of and of which my subtle colleagues, who are in a better position than I to grasp what is happening, have spoken.

The first of these might be thought of as a plumbing problem. Imagine a network of pipes through which water flows. This network is adjusted to handle a particular volume of water. Now increase that flow a hundred-fold. Pipes must widen, new connections need to be formed, and the entire network must expand in order to handle the increased volume.

In Gaia's case, it's not water but living energies of various kinds, which for simplicity's sake we can think of collectively as "Light" whose volume is now increasing. In some cases, the quality or type of this Light is different from anything Gaia has dealt with in the past, so whole new "pipes" or connections need to be put into place. (Imagine that some of the new water in our plumbing metaphor is actually radioactive, requiring different kinds of pipes to contain the radioactivity.)

The main point is that the internal energy ecosystem of Gaia as an organism is becoming more complex and needing to manifest a greater degree of wholeness, coherence, and integration in order to embody and properly process ("metabolize") the new spiritual and cosmic energies it is now receiving.

The second effect of which I am aware is that the new energies are very stimulating, bringing to the surface things that have been buried, hidden, or dormant. Imagine a field that appears empty. Rain comes, and now the seeds that were hidden underground are stimulated to sprout. Many of them produce unexpected and beautiful flowers but some produce noxious and unwanted weeds. The point is that we now know what the field contains and can take steps to nourish the flowers while removing the weeds.

When we think of an influx of Light, we imagine that it stimulates and nourishes only that which is good, but in fact, it brings many things to the surface, even things that are unpleasant. This gives knowledge that provides an opportunity for healing and transformation in order to produce wholeness, but it's an opportunity that needs to be grasped and used.

The Call of Light

As a result of whatever changes are happening in the cosmic environment, the effects of heightened energies within Gaia affect all life on our planet, including Humanity. Much of the turmoil of the past decades can be attributed to the changes within the Gaian subtle ecosystem. In the symbolism of astrology, this is a time of transition from one Age to another, the dawning of Aquarius, with accompanying impacts upon the collective unconscious and consciousness of humanity. These inner effects are in addition to the growing outer, physical problems of a changing planet, most notably seen in the developing climate crisis. It makes for a challenging time, but also a time of opportunity.

I wrote of sensing these changes and their effects as a great storm bearing down upon us, but that is only part of the picture. I lived for several years in San Mateo County on the San Francisco Bay side of the San Francisco Peninsula, a beautiful part of Northern California. This peninsula is a narrow strip of land running between San Jose in the south and San Francisco in the north. The Santa Cruz mountains form a kind of spine dividing the peninsula from the Bay on the one side and the Pacific Ocean on the other.

Quite often, I could look up at this mountain range to the west and see huge banks of white fog pouring over the hilly tops and down into the valley below where I lived. It was always a spectacular sight. It was like a fountain of Light cascading into the world.

This is what I see in the world today with my inner vision, not only storms but an outflow of Light to help Gaia—and us—through this difficult period.

There is a limit, though, to what this Light can do and how helpful it can be. Think of a land that has been through a severe drought. The soil is dry, hard, and packed. A rainstorm can come, dropping buckets of needed water on the land, but because the soil is so dry, it can't assimilate and absorb it. The water runs off, usually in the form of flash floods. The land remains as dry as ever once the sun comes out and the floods recede.

This is especially true where forests have been cut and the land has been deprived of the natural root systems that can capture, hold, and channel the water, giving the soil a chance to absorb it.

The same thing happens with subtle energy "rainfalls" of Light. Unless there are beings who can receive and integrate these new energies, they "run off," perhaps causing disruption in the process. We need to remember that Gaia is an organism, and vital subtle energies flow along and are integrated by ecological networks of subtle organisms (Devas, nature spirits, angels, elementals, and others) as well as by physical ones (plants, animals, and, yes, human beings).

As Gaia is taking on new cosmic energies, there is a need for both subtle and physical partners to step up to help receive, absorb, and integrate these new forces. This is the call of Light in our time. Gaia seeks partners. This call, this need, is what I seek to address in this book.

The Human Energy System

We are all energy processing systems.

We take energy into ourselves in various forms, and we put energy back into the world through our thinking, feeling, and activities. In between the energies we take in and the energies we put out, there is a great deal of physical and subtle processing that takes place.

This is not how we usually think of ourselves, especially not in a spiritual context, but it's a useful perspective when trying to understand the opportunities for Gaian partnership available to us and what may be asked of us. As always, trying to describe non-physical reality in physical terms is difficult—I, at least, don't always have the words I need, and I prefer to stay away from esoteric jargon and out of the occult weeds if I can. So, let me tell it as a story.

My understanding is that the seeds of Humanity came to this world as a gathering, a "clan" or collective consciousness within the Stellar Realms, the same as Gaia. These were beings associated with a variety of stellar Presences—perhaps part of what might be thought of as Gaia's "natural allies" or soul family—and they constituted a soul cluster containing unique properties and qualities to add to Gaia's evolving life and plan as a "star of life." Perhaps metaphorically we might think of this soul cluster—which I shall henceforward refer to as "Cosmic Humanity" to differentiate it from the Planetary Humanity that subsequently evolved here on Earth—as akin to yeast added to dough to help it to rise.

Once Cosmic Humanity had become integrated into the life energies of Gaia—i.e., once the seeds of a Planetary Humanity had been planted—then other beings and consciousnesses not originally part of this ancient stellar soul cluster could also come and choose a path of human development and evolution. The opportunity to partake at least in part of the human experience is open to any being who chooses to undertake it. Still, Cosmic Humanity remains the core structure and patterning of how Gaia and Humanity interweave.

In order for this blending to take place and the seeds to be planted, Cosmic Humanity developed both a "Gaian Sheath," a field of energy uniquely attuned to and part of Gaia, and a "Humanity Sheath," a similar emergent field of collective energy attuned to the particular destiny and role Humanity played, plays, and will play within the Gaian metabolic ecosystem.

Here is a picture:

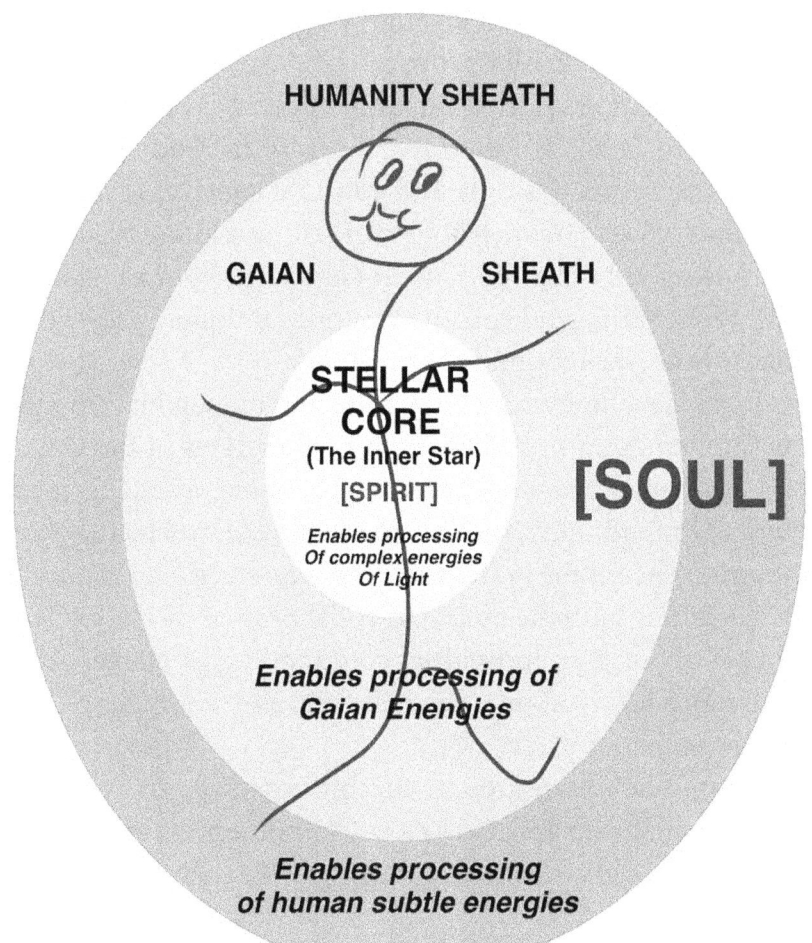

This is the beginning of the human energy system. It is a pattern contained within each of us. Let's explore it a little further in our story.

We never lose our stellar core. This is the star within us. I think of it as our Spirit, our sacred Identity. Because it is naturally and organically part of the Stellar Realm, it always has the capacity to attune to, process, and embody the complex forms, patterns, and energies of Light that exist and operate in that Realm. Its presence within us ultimately provides the foundation through which we can receive and metabolize Light in all its forms.

In a similar way, the Gaian Sheath enables us as energy systems to receive, integrate, work with, and generally process all forms of subtle and spiritual energies associated with the ecology and metabolism of Gaia as a living organism. Likewise, the Humanity Sheath enables us to do the same with those subtle and spiritual energies uniquely associated with human development and activity.

In the development of Humanity and human individuals, the Soul emerges out of the blending energies of the Gaian and Humanity Sheaths, becoming a stable, evolving focal point of individuality, growth and identity. (And by the way, the emergence of the individual soul is rarely, if ever, a purely private affair but takes place in collaborative ways—we are all part of our own individual soul families or clusters.) I'll have more to say about these Sheaths and our Stellar Core further on in our story.

These Sheaths represent the big picture, our personal macrocosm, if you will. On a closer-to-home individual level, our human energy system looks more like this:

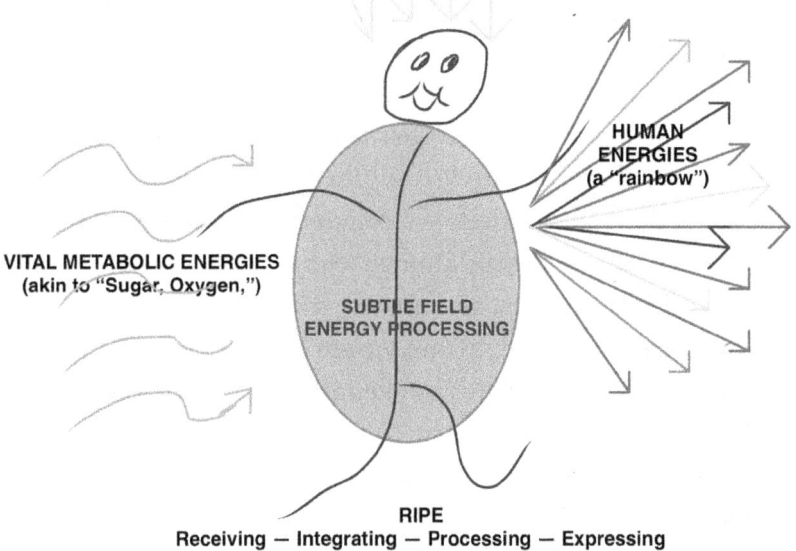

Receiving — Integrating — Processing — Expressing

This is a simplified diagram that shows our energetic potentials and activities, most of which take place below the threshold of conscious awareness, though sensitive and psychic individuals aware of subtle energies can often recognize when these processes are happening.

We each live in a surrounding "soup" of generally nourishing and vitalizing subtle energies that flow through the subtle environment around us. On the whole, these come from planetary and ecosystem Devas and angels, such as the Devas that overlight the mountain ranges around my home and that regularly send invigorating Light and blessing out into the surrounding environment. These energies can also come from more localized nature spirits and elemental beings and even from plants such as trees or other human beings, such as my kindly neighbors. (Yes, there are toxic forces as well, most of which we create for ourselves; we'll discuss them later in the book.) These vital metabolic energies are the subtle equivalent, say, of sugar or oxygen in our physical bloodstream, giving us energy. Our subtle bodies are designed to receive and process these vital streams, though we can certainly block or disrupt the process through our behavior, thinking, and feeling.

At the same time, we are also capable of receiving, integrating, and processing Light energies from higher, more complex dimensions. These are akin to complex molecules that our internal energy system (grounded, we remember, in our Stellar Core whether we are consciously attuned to that Core or not in our daily lives) can learn to digest and absorb, thereby "grounding them" into our incarnate world. In this, we are like the root system I used as an earlier example that can take rainwater and enable the soil to absorb it so it doesn't just run off.

If you'd like another metaphor, then think of our subtle energy system as eating a chocolate candy bar from the subtle environment (yum! Quick energy!) and a full-course meal from the higher levels of Light, which needs time to digest. The important point is that our subtle bodies, which themselves are multi-layered, are designed to handle a wide variety of subtle and spiritual energies moving through and into and around the ecological metabolism of Gaia.

At the same time, as we take these energies in and assimilate them, we transform them and put energies of various kinds and qualities back into the world in a kind of "rainbow" effect (because there's no one single color or kind of energy that most people radiate, it's a wide spectrum from some truly toxic and malignant energies to energies of Light that bless the world).

I describe the process that takes place within the "Black Box" of our subtle energy system with an acronym: RIPE. It stands for Receiving, Integrating, Processing, and Expressing. We'll discuss this in more detail in a moment. But first, there's a third important element to our story.

If you are familiar with Incarnational Spirituality, you'll

recognize the idea of Self-Light (if not, a good place to start is with my book, *Journey into Fire*). Self-Light is an expression of our generative capacity and a vitally important part of who we are as spiritual and subtle energy individuals.

We do not only receive and process subtle and spiritual energies or Light from our surroundings or from higher levels of life. We generate it as well. As I've been saying, we are ourselves individual "stars of life," and like a star in the cosmos, we generate energy. This star-like quality ultimately rests upon and emerges from our ancient Stellar Core, but it also emerges in our everyday lives as a result of the soul's incarnational process and engagement with the incarnate realm of body, mind, emotion, and subtle energy.

Self-Light is not all that we radiate, of course. I have felt the almost physical pain of bolts of angry subtle energy hitting my subtle body, like fiery red arrows, and I have felt the calming, uplifting touch of a blessing or a loving energy that someone has sent to me. As I mentioned above, we give out a variety of subtle and spiritual energies depending on the overall quality of our incarnate life and on our thinking, feeling, emoting, and acting in the moment.

Of course, I have a picture for this:

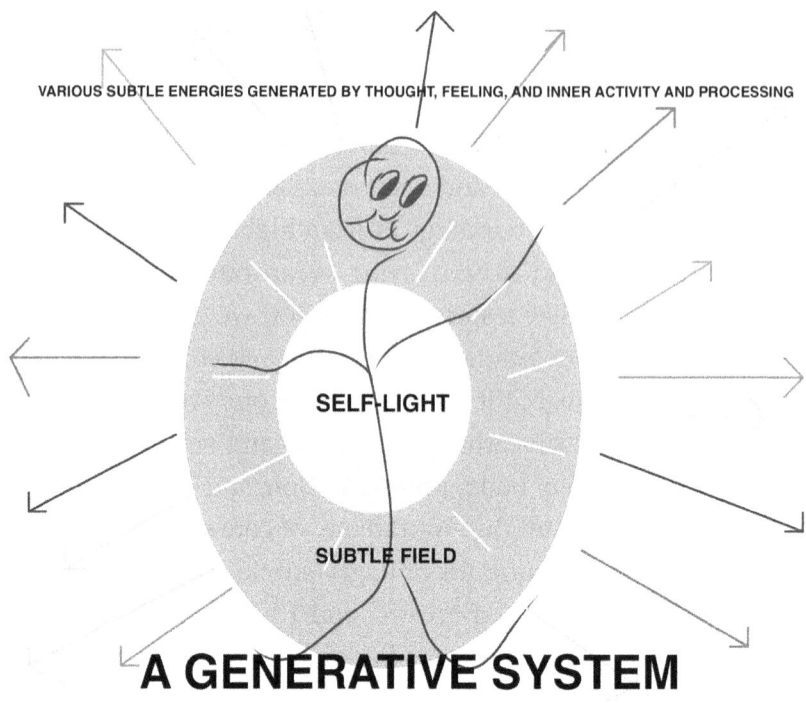

A GENERATIVE SYSTEM

This story simplifies a great deal and leaves a lot out, but as I said earlier, I'm not writing a book on the esoteric of our subtle anatomy and physiology. What I am trying to do is establish a context for understanding how and why we can partner with Gaia in ways that meet the needs of our historical moment. Having some appreciation for ourselves as complex and powerful energy systems is an important component of this context and understanding.

RIPE

RIPE stands for **R**eceiving, **I**ntegrating, **P**rocessing, and **E**xpressing subtle and spiritual energies. It's a simple description of our own internal subtle energetic metabolic process. While a person can be conscious of this process and even influence it in various ways, most people are likely not. People's attention just doesn't go to the subtle realms in ways that would bring these processes to their awareness. The subtle worlds remain invisible and unknown to them, both in their surroundings and within themselves.

But this doesn't mean that these energetic realms do not exist nor that these processes are not occurring. Indeed, where these processes are disrupted or obstructed and energy does not circulate in healthy ways within and around us, our lives can be much poorer for it.

RIPE describes a way (one way, others are possible) of engaging and working with subtle forces and energies, ways of expressing our human energy system. For a long time, as a simple approach, I simply said that we had the capacity to hold subtle energies and that we needed to learn how to do so successfully. Holding is very important, but this was an incomplete and overly simplistic description. We are more than just passive containers. We don't "hold" the way a glass holds water. We "hold" the way a body contains its metabolic, physiological energy. Holding as a subtle energy concept represents something dynamic, and RIPE is a way of describing that dynamism.

Receiving usually means that something has landed in our consciousness, and we are now aware of it. We perceive it. It is a combination energetically of attunement, sensitivity, resonance, intention, and, often most important, attention. However, the mere fact of awareness doesn't always mean that we receive something in the sense that we accept it and can now act upon it or with it. There is an old joke about the wife (or husband) who says, "He (she) doesn't hear me, even when I'm speaking to him (her)."

Earlier in this book, I told the story of having a bad case of measles when I was six that damaged the hearing nerves in my brain. As a result, I have been partly deaf all of my life since then. I don't hear most bird songs, for instance, as it is at a pitch that's outside my range of hearing. I may know that birds are singing, as my wife Julia tells me how beautiful they are in the morning, but I cannot receive their song into my consciousness.

With the subtle dimension, though, things can be different. I may not consciously feel the play of various subtle energies on my subtle body, but the intelligence within my subtle body is aware and can receive those energies into my subtle energy system. It can do so if it has resonance, alignment or attunement, and sympathy with those energies. Other energies may pass through me or by me, and I do not have the sensitivity to receive or even be aware of them.

It's like being a radio. If I'm attuned to a particular station, I will receive whatever music or information is being broadcast over that frequency. If I want something different, then I need to "change the dial" and attune to a different station.

The Call of Light in our time is asking us to learn to receive into our energy systems whole new frequencies of Light. Maybe this sounds like an impossible task, but we may find it is easier to do than we expect, or at least within the realm of possibility. The reason is our Stellar Core. When it comes to higher frequencies of Light, it knows what the rest of us may have forgotten or not yet learned.

As we shall see as we proceed, often it is intention and attention that are most important in helping us receive subtle energies. And we have other help as well.

Integrating is the next part of the RIPE process. To integrate is to take in what we're receiving and make it part of ourselves. It's a matter of absorption, digestion, and assimilation. When, in the old joke, the wife (or husband) says, "He (she) hears me, but he (she) doesn't listen," they're talking about integration. Nothing has been taken in where it makes a difference.

Within the subtle and spiritual worlds, often the greatest asset to integration is silence. Rather than bombarding the new information or energy with "digestive juices" of analysis, questioning, doubt, comparison, and so forth, trying to tear it apart and break it down, one may simply need to just sit with the new experience, the new energy, and let it speak in its own way and its own timing. Integration takes on the character of a conversation. This is possible because all subtle and spiritual energies are themselves alive and sentient; they possess their own kind of intelligence which seeks to blend and integrate with our own to allow something new to emerge.

Silence and just sitting and listening can require courage and trust, especially trust in oneself. An important element of integration is acceptance. I accept this into myself, which can be more challenging if it's a quality or energy with which we are not familiar. We can become anxious, even fearful, and stop the integration process, to say nothing of the receiving.

To integrate something is to allow it to become one with us, part of us, not necessarily permanently but certainly as part of a dynamic process in the moment. We can always say *"No"* which is one of our human "superpowers." We *can* say no to subtle and spiritual energies and not allow them entry into our lives. Learning to say *"Yes"* in powerful, trusting, and wise ways, however, opens doors that can bless the world.

Processing means that once we have integrated something and taken it into ourselves, we do something with it. Transformation occurs. Here is where the process has similarities to physical digestion, the act of turning a food—something that is "not us"—into our own flesh—something that now is "us." That French fry I just ate was once a root lying snug in the soil, and now it is becoming part of my cellular matter.

When it comes to subtle and spiritual energies, we process in a variety of ways. We can turn the inspiration of an energy we are integrating into thoughts, ideas, plans, visions, and opinions. Subtle spiritual energies can turn into an emotion, or a feeling, inspire me to love, or inspire hate, give me courage, or give me fear.

Subtle energies can be processed into physical healing or into a sense of vitality. On the other hand, if they are toxic, they can have the opposite effect, one that is deleterious to our health and well-being (and perhaps, unfortunately, that of those around us).

Expressing can turn processing into action. Expressing is when I do something in my world. I turn my energy outward into behavior, which is often vitally necessary to actually connect my energy with the world so that I become part of a greater flow of Gaian energy circulation. Energy held within myself can become stagnant and back up, clogging the system.

A very simple exercise of energy expression as part of RIPE is the Incarnational Spirituality exercise called the Touch of Love. This exercise is presented here again as a reminder of its powerful impact both on a personal environment level and in the practice of becoming a part of the flow of Gaian energies.

Touch of Love Exercise

- Fill yourself with your Self-Light and with a felt sense of lovingness. You might imagine, for instance, your heart overflowing with love or your spine glowing with love. Express the highest form of love that you can authentically feel in your whole being—body, mind, heart, energy, and soul—right now.

- Feel this love flowing out from the core of your being, down your arms and into your hands. Feel this love pooling in your fingertips.

- Reach out and touch something. As you do so, feel the love in your fingertips overflowing. In this Touch of Love, you do not take anything into yourself. You do not really project it into anything either. You simply let it pool in your fingertips and overflow, allowing that which you touch to absorb it in its own way.

- As love flows through your touch, it also stirs and flows and circulates through your own being, bringing love to all parts of yourself just as you are bringing it to the things you touch.
- Likewise, as love flows through your touch, it also stirs and flows and circulates through your environment, rippling out in waves from the things you touch, expanding the influence of your loving touch.
- Feel this expanding, circulating love bringing the blessing and empowering vitality of your Self-Light into your environment.
- When you feel finished, just remove your fingers and allow the love to be absorbed into all parts of your body.

As noted previously and again worth repeating, we touch each other's incarnations all the time. The energies we project to each other, the way we think of each other, the feelings we surround others with, the looks we give, the tones of voice, the words we use; all of these are touches. But are they touches that help us to incarnate and help the incarnation of another, or do they hinder and obstruct? That is what only we can determine. We can remember, though, that a silent partnership of blessing is always at our real—and virtual— fingertips.

The important thing here is that we are circulating our subtle and spiritual energies, taking part in the metabolism and ecology of the living world of Gaia around us.

However we do it—and there are so, so many ways, including all acts of goodwill and kindness—giving expression to the Light and subtle energies within us is a necessary component of RIPE, and one that can truly make a difference.

This is just a simple overview of the RIPE principle. I think a small book could probably be written exploring its various components. We will certainly be revisiting this concept again and again in the material that is yet to come. There is much here that repays attention and contemplation.

Before we leave this RIPE discussion, though, there is one final important point. What truly makes RIPE work and what underlies the health and success of our subtle energy nature is love. We receive with love, we integrate with love, we process with love, we express with love. Love is the foundation. If we understand this, we have the key that opens the treasures and wonders of our human energy system, allowing us to stand as partners with Gaia and all her angels and Devas. Then we bless the world!

The Entelechy

In ecology, organisms are considered "coupled" with their environment; that is, the nature and functioning of an organism is tied into the nature of its environment and the connections it forms with that ecosystem. When an organism is taken out of its environment and studied in isolation, as in a laboratory, information can be obtained but it is never complete. It cannot give a whole picture. A mouse adapted to the American desert Southwest and one whose home is in the boreal forests of Canada are both rodents, but they are not the same. Each has characteristics that evolved to adapt to its particular native ecosystem. Without understanding where the mouse comes from, a particular characteristic may be overlooked or misunderstood.

Human beings are among the most highly adaptable life forms on Earth, able to survive and even thrive in a variety of ecosystems. This is true on a subtle energetic level as well. But the fact remains that wherever we are, our natural subtle energy system is coupled with the subtle environment around it. In a way, that's the point. In the subtle world, connection is often the name of the game as we are here to add to the wholeness of Gaia, not take away from it. Our subtle energy field is an instrument of connectedness and wholeness, as well as of energy exchange and processing.

In my life, I have moved around a great deal and lived in various parts of the world. I was born in Ohio, grew up in Morocco, went to high school first at Deerfield Academy in Old Deerfield, Massachusetts, then later at West High in Phoenix, Arizona. I've lived in California, Wisconsin, Scotland, and here in the Pacific Northwest, near Seattle. In each of these places, the subtle environment was different. I learned to make connections with it and with the subtle beings native to that invisible ecosystem, and I felt that each place became "home."

In some ways, my "energy identity" changed depending on the nature of the subtle environment around me. For instance, living in Old Deerfield, the world felt cozy, and my energy field felt tighter around me, closer to home, so to speak. But when we moved to Phoenix and I was exposed to the Arizona desert, I felt my energy field expand and become more spacious, matching the openness and spaciousness around me.

However, through all these changes, there was also a sense of a consistent subtle environment around me that had nothing to do with where I was living but was a field of support arising from a group of subtle beings intimately associated with my incarnation. In some ways, it was akin to feeling the presence of my Mom and Dad. Wherever we moved in the world, from Ohio to California to Morocco to Massachusetts and Arizona, they were always there, creating a consistent field of love and support. (I was blessed with such great parents!)

Each of us has such a mobile environment of subtle love and support around us that acts as a kind of extension of our personal energy field. Earlier in this book, I called this field the product of our "natural allies" or our *Entelechy.*

As I wrote earlier, the word *Entelechy* (or *entelecheia*) was coined by the Greek philosopher Aristotle to describe the motion of potentiality into actuality and manifestation that defines a being. I am using it to refer to our natural allies, as collectively these beings work together to help bring the potentiality of an incarnation into actuality and create a unique subtle environment tailored to our personal incarnation. Our Entelechy extends and supports our personal energy field in powerful ways to engage with Gaia's ecology and metabolism around us.

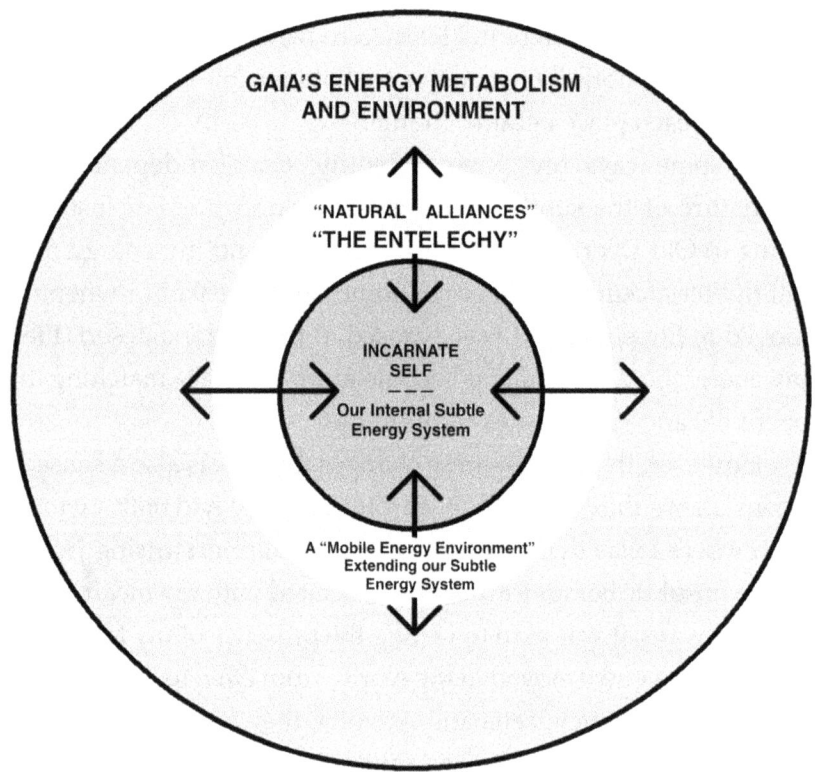

Our Entelechy is made up of a group of beings such as the Body Intelligence, the Incarnational Elemental (which I previously called the "Body Elemental"), the Guardian Angel, and our Pit Crew, all of whom are intimately associated with our incarnation. We are "coupled" together. Wherever we may go in the world, whatever particular local subtle environment and ecosystem we become part of, our Entelechy is there with us.

The Gaian Human

For a number of years now, the non-physical beings with whom I work and whom I call variously my "subtle colleagues" or my "Pit Crew," have spoken of changes taking place in the structure and functioning of the subtle body we create when we incarnate (a creation, by the way, assisted and contributed to by members of our Entelechy). They have talked about the emergence of a "new subtle body," one more attuned to Gaia, with a greater capacity for forming the connections necessary to participate in the Gaian metabolism and ecology and to enhance Gaian wholeness. Such an emergence, they said, was vital to the survival and thriving of humanity going forward, as it was a necessary adaptation to the planetary changes taking place.

It's one thing to be told—and to sense in one's own being—that such changes are happening, but it's something else again to understand them, much less to be able to write about them. I could accept what my subtle colleagues were telling me and still not have any real insight into just what it meant or how a new subtle body would manifest differently. As physical individuals, we generally lack both the conceptual basis and the language to explain non-physical, multi-dimensional phenomena. It's been my experience in such circumstances, as I alluded to above, that if I want to integrate new information, it's often best just to sit with it and give it time to unpack and reveal itself in its own way. Not trying to understand can be the route towards understanding.

An experience I had contacting our ancient Stellar Core, our Cosmic Humanity, provided the key that began to unlock some (though hardly all) of the mystery behind the emergence of a new human subtle body. This leads us in our story to something I'm now calling the "Gaian Human."

When one of our daughters was sixteen, she went to Thailand as a foreign exchange student for a year. For the first three months of her trip, she was not allowed to contact us, nor could we contact her other than once a month. The purpose was to give her the time and space to become fully immersed in her new culture, language, and home, and to minimize homesickness and distraction. In effect, a veil was drawn between us to allow our daughter to accomplish a task successfully which she did with flying colors. It wasn't easy, but it was necessary.

Let's go back to the earlier discussion of the Stellar Core and the two Sheaths, the Gaian Sheath and the Humanity Sheath. Only now, I wish to add a new element to the picture I drew then - the Veil.

What is important to understand is that, like our daughter in Thailand, each of the two Sheaths needed space and opportunity to develop their own unique character in a new environment. It was necessary that the Gaian Sheath not simply be a reflection of the influences and nature of the Stellar Realm, as embodied in the Stellar Core of Humanity (and of each of us). Likewise, it was important that the Humanity Sheath not simply reflect and mimic the influences and character of Gaia. In each case, a unique identity needed to evolve.

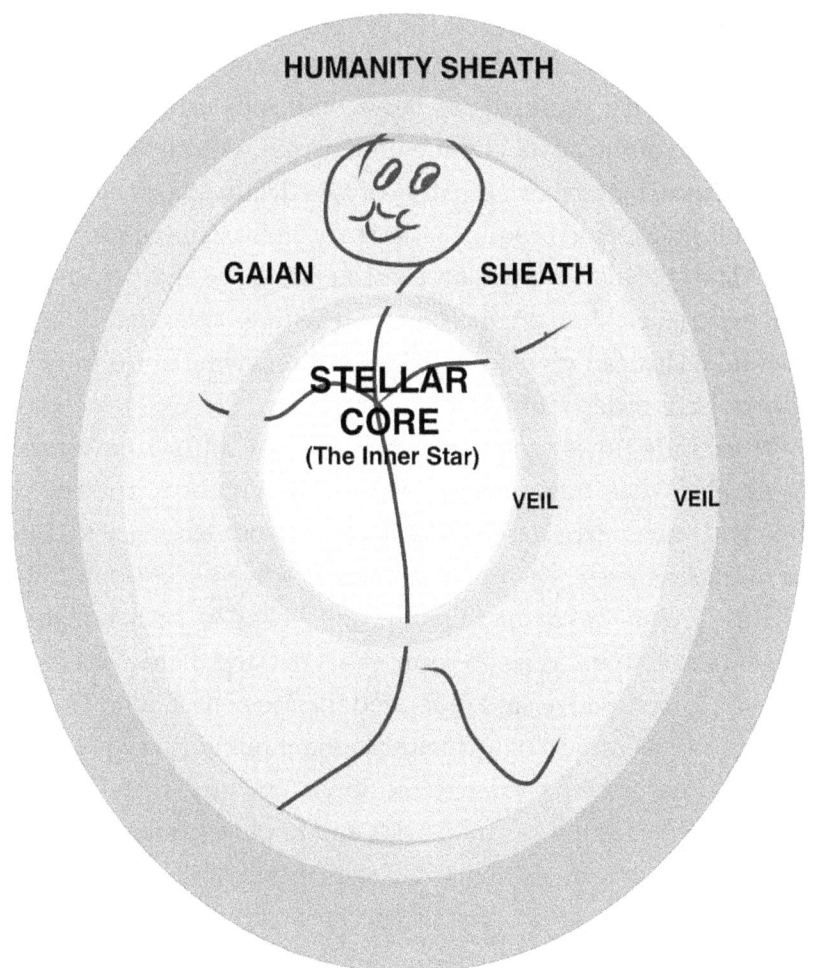

To accomplish this, "veils" were inserted between the Sheaths to diminish or even in some cases cut off the transmission of energies from one layer to another. This was not an absolute cutting off. These veils are more like cell membranes, permeable to some influences but blocked to others. They were adapted to what was needed at the time to allow for the proper development within each of the Sheaths. But it did create a condition in which the wholeness of Gaia was subordinated to local needs.

My understanding is that the effect of these veils was closely observed and monitored, but the consequences could not always be predicted in advance. There is randomness and chance involved in evolutionary processes as new conditions can produce the emergence of the novel and the unexpected. Who would expect, for instance, that the combination of two deadly poisons, sodium and chloride, would produce a necessary life-sustaining substance: salt? The spiritual worlds don't resist emergence and surprise; in my experience, they often celebrate it with wonder and delight. A little chaos can give a vitalizing and renewing spice to what otherwise is orderly and predictable.

But sometimes, consequences take an unfortunate turn, especially when human consciousnesses, with our capacity for free will and unexpected choices, as well as our tendency to cling to old habits even when they no longer serve us, enter into the picture. Human behavior, thinking, and feeling began to add their own "noise" to the veils, in some cases making them even more obscured, obstructive, and separated than they needed to be. The membranes became clogged with stagnant human energies.

Now, unforeseen barriers to the flow of energies and wholeness between the Sheaths began to arise and to persist, increasing the separation between elements of Gaia's metabolism and ecology. To use colorful language, the veils became corrupted with "gunk."

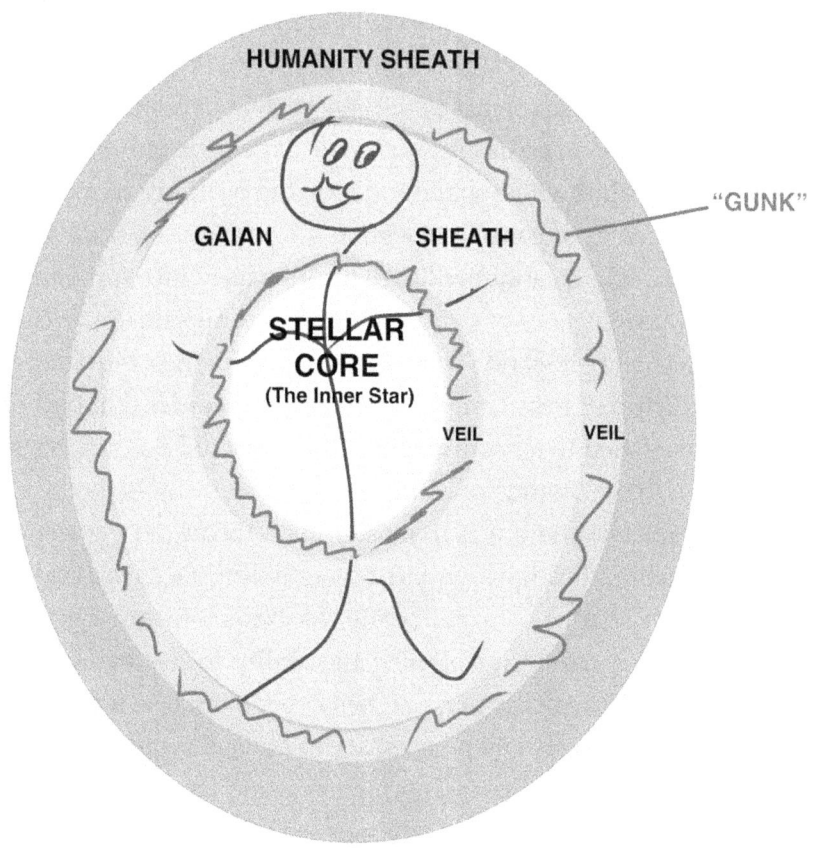

One reason for this condition has to do with a necessary part of the evolution of a part of Cosmic/Planetary Humanity. For much of Humanity's existence, we incarnated in a vibrationally heightened form of subtle matter, not in the denser physical world with which we are familiar now. However, physical matter—or what may be called the Elemental of Matter—has capacities and wisdoms that part of Humanity, at least, wished to learn and master. This required taking on full physical incarnation. This descent from a higher vibrational world was not a "Fall," as some mythologies present it (though given the effects that transpired, one can understand how this process could be interpreted as such). It was a deliberate movement of consciousness from one dimension to another, with Gaian, Devic, and angelic help. But such changes are not without a price.

Two of the characteristics of the energy field of physical matter may be described as *persistence of structure* and *permanence*. Unlike in the subtle realms where shape and form can be fluid and relevant to inner processes of consciousness, in the physical world, a rock is a rock is a rock. It cannot willingly change itself into something else. It has a persistence of structure—unless some outside force is applied to change it—and it has relative permanence, depending on that structure. These, among others, were qualities that part of Humanity wished to learn and master so as not to be as subject as it had been to the "winds of change."

The real lesson here was to master these forces of persistence and permanence through love and intentionality; it was to develop the power to change as a deliberate, conscious, creative act. In simple terms, it meant developing the ability to use habits and routine as a useful infrastructure when needed but also the ability to change those habits when necessary to move forward. The risk was to get trapped in states of permanence and habit, resisting or being unable to effect change; the reward was to gain a greater capacity for creativity and emergence.

Two twin challenges for incarnate humanity in this situation were inertia and laziness; it became easier to go with a habit than to try to change it unless forced by outside pressures. I think we've all experienced this in personal ways in our lives. True change is work! But where Humanity was concerned, it meant that habits of collective behavior, often embodied in cultural beliefs, mores, and thought-forms, persisted long after they were useful.

Think of the many wars and acts of violence in the world perpetuated by people against others based on outworn beliefs (the belief in the effectiveness of violence itself being one of the most outworn habits of all). Tribes and nations war with each other because this is their habit of behavior over many centuries, and the will to change it constantly runs up against inertia and the power of permanence and persistence.

In other words, humanity created habits and mental, emotional structures ("thought-forms") of "gunk," and these persisted over time, often growing in strength (or at least deepening in inertia), corrupting the veils and making them more obstructive and separative than they ever needed or were intended to be.

One good example of this which is bedeviling the modern world is the loss of the sense of Gaia as a living organism, a living being. This awareness took different forms among people and collectively is known as *animism*, the idea that everything, including the planet itself, is alive. But in modern technological society, West and East, this idea has been lost or replaced by the image of the world (and the cosmos itself) as nothing more than a machine run by blind, random forces. This thought-form—a truly pernicious and weird form of subtle "gunk"—is largely responsible for the arising of a civilization—ours—that is steadily and blindly destroying the ecological wholeness of the world and precipitating a transformative climate crisis that conceivably could lead to the extinction of most current life on earth, including us.

It is a case of the Humanity Sheath being dangerously cut off from the Gaian Sheath (to say nothing of the Stellar Core at the heart of all of it).

Another, even more challenging form of "gunk" obscuring the connections between the Sheaths and the Core, is the persistence of trauma. Humanity has a talent for generating trauma, both individual and collective suffering and pain. Some of this is immediate, affecting the current life, but other traumas persist through generations of people, seemingly intractable and beyond healing because they have become buried deep or woven into the very structure of what we consider the way of things. Of particular note in this area is the trauma that exists between men and women, gender and sexual trauma that has a way of persisting and repeating itself, or the trauma that has now collected around racial relationships or religious rivalries. It's one thing to suffer and then let it go, allowing the body, mind, and soul to heal and renew itself. It's something else again for that suffering to become part of our physical collective and social "muscle memory," taking on a dreadful permanence in our thinking, feeling, and behaving. This is truly major "gunk" clogging up the human side, at least, of the Gaian ecology and metabolism.

It may be wondered and asked why this happened and how the spiritual forces of the world permitted it. It's because evolution is not a straight line of unending and inevitable progress but a meandering oscillation between error and correction, missteps and full steps, retreats and advances. On the whole, the arc moves towards wholeness and the fulfillment of Gaia's purpose as a star of life.

The fact is that the spiritual forces are working—and have always been working—to keep things on track. It doesn't always seem like it because Humanity can be a hard case, reluctant to change as a collective. But great efforts have been made to prevent the gunk from closing the veils. The planetary redemptive effort of the Christ is one such example, which permanently opened pathways through the veils and the gunk for those able and willing to take them (and not necessarily religious pathways; energetic paths which sometimes become themselves subject to corruption and the acquisition of "gunk"). There are many other examples, great and small.

Humanity is a vast collective energy field that is slow to change, like a huge ocean-going container ship. It carries with it a mass of inertia from past habits, thoughts, beliefs, and actions. Seen from that scale, it may seem an impossible task to get it to change unless forced to do so by extreme and dangerous circumstances.

But container ships and other large vessels can be steered; otherwise, they would never reach their intended destinations.

This is accomplished by large rudders capable of changing the direction of the vessel. But such rudders are themselves so large as to possess inertia. What enables them to overcome this and turn are smaller rudders built into them, called *trimtabs*. These trimtabs are small enough that it doesn't take anywhere near the same kind of power to enable them to turn against the force of the ocean current created by the movement of the vessel. Once they turn, the larger rudder can turn, and once it turns, the boat turns.

Each of us is a human trimtab for the vessel of Humanity.

The whole point of this book is that the spiritual forces working with Gaia and Humanity cannot by themselves enable the changes that need to take place. Like huge rudders, they require partnership with individuals, with you and me. We have the power to make the changes which they can then amplify, like force multipliers, to bring change to Humanity as a whole. It may still be a slow process. Container ships don't stop and turn on a dime! But it's a directed process, heading towards the desired destination.

And it depends on us. It depends on our capacity to partner with spiritual allies on behalf of Gaia and Humanity.

This brings me back to the idea of the Gaian Human. The Gaian Human is the person whose Stellar Core and Gaian and Humanity Sheaths are once again resonating in harmony and communicating with each other. There may still be some veils there—we are not yet ready for full immersion in Gaia's life nor in the power of the Stellar Realms—but they will be more transparent and translucent than before. We will see through the "glass" more clearly and experience the wholeness of ourselves and of Gaia more organically and deeply. We will be freer of the gunk and able to extend that freedom into the human collective.

The Gaian Human is the trimtab of the future; it turns the collective human vessel in the right direction. It's a trimtab built of individual initiative, love, intentionality, freedom, and connection—and of partnership with our subtle environment and the spiritual forces of Gaia. It is the individual standing in her or his sacredness and in communion and collaboration with the Gaian life within the environment.

We have tools to bring the Sheaths and the Stellar Core of our being into closer communion. Now we need to use them.

To some extent, the emergence of this new subtle body in which Core and Sheaths are in greater communication is happening naturally. It has to as a response and an adaptation to the fact that the gunk is being removed and the veils are thinning on a global human level, largely in response to the stimulation of the incoming new cosmic energies that are demanding a greater level of wholeness in response. Bringing Humanity's gunk, often long buried in the shadows and mysteries of the Veils and in the subconscious of our species, is not a pleasant process, drawing much to the surface to be confronted, challenged, transformed, and healed. No wonder there is so much turmoil in the human world these days! But it is happening, and it affects us as individuals. Quickly or slowly, easily or with challenge, depending on our responses, it is happening in us.

However, this is not a process with which we can just ride along, making no personal efforts to align with it and change. To be successful requires willing, conscious, loving human cooperation. It requires our own internal efforts to change and to bring greater Light and wholeness into our lives, to blend our own Sheaths and to touch our own Core. And it means aligning those efforts in partnership with our inner allies and the allies of Gaia as well.

There are many ways of becoming a Gaian Human. Based on my experiences with the subtle worlds, in this book I am suggesting one way—a way, frankly, that I am still learning as well but one that seems to be working.

One thing I do know for certain: however we become and are a Gaian Human, it will be an expression of our individual sacredness, our uniqueness, and never a copy of anyone else. One reason "Gaian Human" cannot be rigorously defined is that each of us is—or will be—a unique expression of it. We define it through the lens of our life. How could it be otherwise? We are each "coupled" with our life environment (and with our personal Entelechy) in our own individual way. We each bring something special to the world, something no one else can offer. We each come as a gift to Gaia and to the incarnate world.

It is with the idea of this Gift that we begin our path into becoming a Gaian Human.

The Gift

In the late sixties, as part of the ongoing training my subtle colleague and mentor, "John," was giving me in working with subtle beings and energies, he asked me to do a stint as a psychic counselor, offering people "readings." At first, I was reluctant. I was not confident of my ability to tune in to information that would be helpful to a client. I saw my strengths as a teacher rather than as a counselor. But John persuaded me that it would be a good experience, that he would be helping me, and that it would give me some needed training. So, I agreed, and for the next five or six months, I "hung out my shingle" as someone willing to give intuitive readings.

It was a mixed experience, to say the least. I was, I admit, naively expecting questions on spiritual development, an exploration of how a person might bring greater Light into their lives. Instead, questions ranged from "Can you tell me if I should keep paying the insurance premiums on my ex-husband in case he dies, and I can inherit the money?" to "How can I find a girlfriend?" or "Why don't people like me very much?" Even John was flummoxed by some of the questions, to which his standard reply was, "Well, that's something for you to figure out at your level of consciousness." Needless to say, not every client was happy with the results!

There was, however, one question that came up more frequently than any other, and that was this: "What am I here for? What is the purpose of my life?" People were looking for a North Star that would provide direction in their lives. Or they simply were asking for their life to be validated and given worth, assured that their incarnation and existence on the earth was meaningful.

In some cases, John and I could discern a clear purpose as to why the client's soul had taken incarnation and what it hoped to achieve. But more often than not, there was no such overriding destiny. What was there was a presence of love that wished to offer a blessing to the world through becoming incarnate and sharing the joys and challenges of physical life. Their souls were offering themselves as a gift of Light. It was up to the personality to decide just what form that gift might take.

Forty years later, I was unexpectedly contacted by a member of a subtle race of humans calling themselves the Sidhe (pronounced *shee*). This contact, initiated by a woman named Mariel, led to the production of a card deck and several books of conversations between her and myself.

In one of these conversations, Mariel introduced the idea of *anwa*. *Anwa* meant "gift," specifically the soul gift or inner gift that every living thing offers from itself as its contribution to the wholeness of life. To the Sidhe, *anwa* was at the core, the heart of every incarnation, whether of a stone, a plant, a building, a mountain, a forest, or a person.

In the years of subtle research I have done into the processes of incarnation, this idea of the inner Gift of the soul that each of us brings into incarnate life has loomed large. It was as if the soul were saying, "For I so love the world that I offer myself as a blessing to Gaia and to Humanity." In many ways, it's a deeper, more profound idea than simply that of having a purpose or mission. It speaks more to who we are, and to our identity than to what we do. Especially in the Western world, we so often identify ourselves with our jobs. Unless we have a job, we can feel purposeless, an affliction that can hit men and women who retire and then don't know who they are anymore.

From a mystical standpoint, it could be said that God, the Beloved, (or as I like to say, the "Generative Mystery" behind and within all that is) is the ultimate Gift in creation, the Gift of being and sacredness at the heart of the cosmos. This Gift doesn't have to do anything; it simply is, and that makes everything else possible.

For a particular incarnation, the Gift might be something simple and straightforward. The soul wishes to offer its Light into the world. Or it could be something more complex. It might indeed involve one or more specific purposes or roles that the incarnate personality may undertake. For instance, the soul may feel a Gift of love, compassion, and healing, and this translates into becoming a doctor or a healer in that incarnation. The point is that the Gift speaks to who we are, our sacred identity, from which specific actions emerge. We are free and empowered as to how we present our Gift to the world. If one purpose or avenue of expression doesn't work out, we can try another. A Gift cannot fail in the way a mission can; it is always there to be given. We are always who we are as sacred individuals even if what we want to do doesn't always work out.

Let's look back at the original picture I drew of the Stellar Core and the two Sheaths and change it a bit:

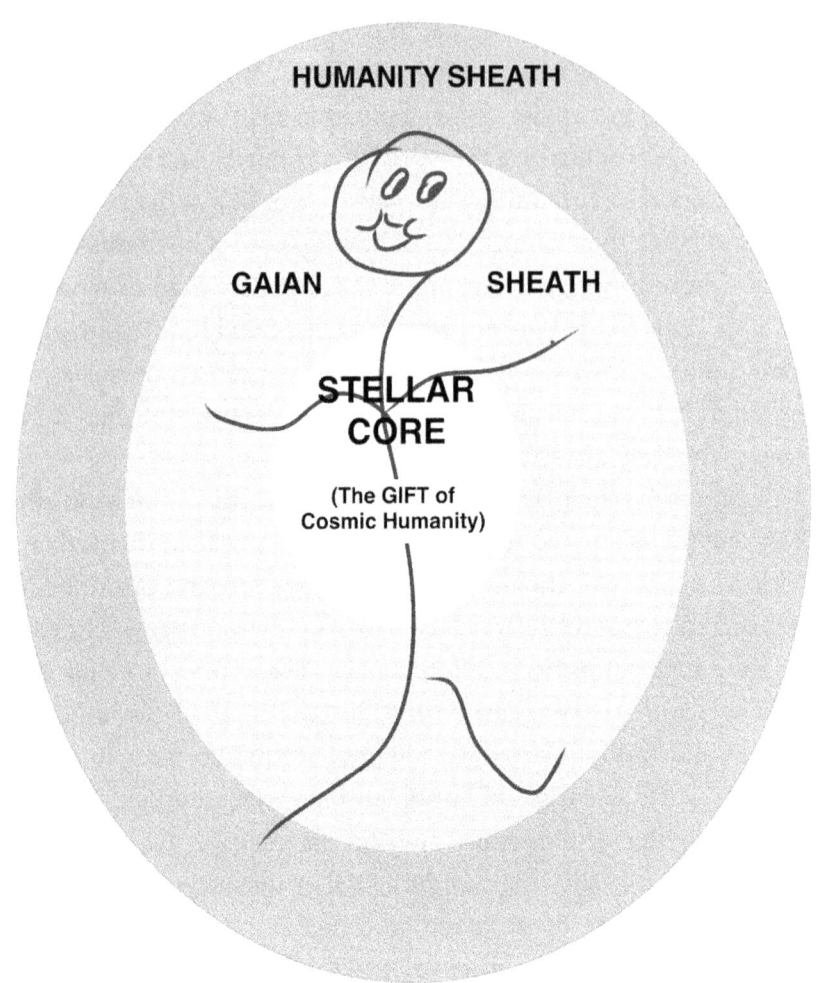

Here we can see that what I am calling the "Stellar Core" could also be called the *anwa* or the Gift of Cosmic Humanity. This Gift is the sum total of qualities and energies that are uniquely part of Cosmic (i.e., Stellar) Humanity and which it collectively brings into the life of Gaia. All our other soul Gifts, simple or complex, that we bring into incarnation are ultimately fractals or manifestations of this primal Gift, our Stellar Gift to a Star of Life.

Do I have thoughts about what the Gift of Cosmic Humanity is? In a small way, about as much as I can tell when it has snowed on the mountaintops around the valley where I live, but from my distant perspective, I can't tell what kind of snow it is or how deep it is or what the contours of the land are underneath it. Much there is a mystery, but a few things do stand out.

The first of these is the quality of love. There are other beings who have entered into the flow of human evolution that bring other important qualities, such as will or intelligence, but the original Cosmic Humanity came with a gift of love.

The second is freedom, embodied as the ability to choose, to make plans, to discover new directions, to foster emergence.

The third strikes me as a quality of creative imagination and the power of introducing novelty (and, when useful, some creative chaos as well). This is an ability to help shape the future, to not only follow a plan but at some point, to become a collaborator and co-designer of that plan as well.

These are the three qualities that stand out to me at the current state of my research as quintessentially human Gifts, born of the original Gift of Cosmic Humanity. There are undoubtedly others that will reveal themselves as Planetary Humanity earns the capacity to perceive, receive, and integrate them.

We touch into the Gift of Cosmic Humanity through our own soul in which it is reflected and embodied. Within the soul, in turn, this Gift of cosmic Light and love becomes translated into the specific soul Gift that becomes our *anwa* at the heart of our incarnation.

I have found that it can be a challenge for people to think of themselves as Gifts of their sacredness, offered to life. This is especially true if the incarnation is a difficult one, filled with hardship or suffering. A person may feel themselves a failure—I know there have been times when I have, and most people in my experience do at one time or another. But outer circumstances do not determine whether we are a Gift of soul and Light or not. That is ultimately who we are, whatever our physical life may be like.

For this reason, I find it useful and important as a daily practice to tune into the Gift, the *anwa*, of our incarnation. It is the beginning of the practice I call the Path, which we'll discuss in detail in a moment and which I have found to be a key practice in partnering with subtle and spiritual beings. The practice puts us in touch with a source of Light within us, and if we allow it, with joy and love. This can transform how we think of ourselves, not in any special or narcissistic way but as a person of value who has something wonderful to contribute to the Commonwealth of Planetary Life. It puts us in touch with our greater Life, our soul life, that enfolds and embraces our personality in an inner partnership and wholeness.

How do we begin to do this? How do we touch into ourselves as a Gift, especially if we have never done so before? Let me share how I do this. It's not the only way, of course, but perhaps it will illustrate the process and give insights into just what the Gift is.

My experience of the Gift is a felt sense, an intention, that I express to myself in this way: "My intent, my desire, is to empower people with love so that they feel the freedom, the worth, and the sovereignty of their innate, individual sacredness, and through that felt sense of empowerment, are able and willing to contribute to the healing and wholeness of the world."

Yes, it's a mouthful!

But this lives in me as a deep commitment and as a feeling. It is who I am. It's like a mission statement, though frankly, it's more of an identity statement. Everything I have done and will continue to do flows from this intent, the Gift I am and wish to give. Thinking of it when I rise in the morning and as I go through my day, puts an inner smile on my face. In fact, my friend and colleague, the most excellent English spiritual teacher, William Bloom, refers to this inner Gift as our inner Smile, that which uplifts us and brings us joy to think about or to attune to.

But a Gift need not take the form of words or anything so elaborate. It's an energy, not a thought-form. It's our core energy, tied into our Soul and ultimately to our Stellar Core, the Presence and Gift of our Cosmic Humanity. Although, as I have done to write about it, we might express it in psychological terms, it's not a mental or emotional construct; it's deeper than that. It is the core energy - the active, sacred Light of our being.

Attuning to it can take practice and can be an act of imagination, but it transcends imagination. That is, it's not who we imagine or would like ourselves to be, though such a self-image might be a place to start. It is who we are at the heart of our incarnation—it is our *anwa*.

Attuning to it might begin with a mantra like, "God is Love, I am love," or "I am here to bring Light and Love into the world." The Gift is an intent, and our power lies in the fact that we can embody such an intent. We can *be* a presence of Sacredness (and in my assuring you of this, you can probably tell that I am expressing my own Gift).

There is nothing in my experience of my Gift—or you of yours—that guarantees its fulfillment. I have an intent to empower people by reminding them of their sacredness, but this doesn't automatically mean I'll do a good job of it, or any job of it at all. I can forget that I am a Gift. I can misunderstand it at a personality level. My sense of my Gift is that it's all about freedom and liberation from anything that binds us and prevents us from experiencing our sacredness, but I could translate that into a teaching or dogma that ends up doing the opposite.

There is a way in which the personality and its vision and desires melts in the presence of the Gift and surrenders to a higher sense of who and what we are; there is also an equally important way in which our personality provides the concrete, expressive means for translating the Gift we are into practical service and engagement with the world. Part of the challenge of incarnation is getting this balance right, which can take experience and practice.

In this context, one important aspect of the Gift is that, as a

Gift—as an expression of something freely and lovingly given—it is not transactional. The Gift is not given in order to get something in return. That creates a closed system. A Gift creates an open system, one open to novelty and emergence. The Sacred, the Gift at the heart of creation, asks nothing in return for being, and as a result, it receives everything. If I'm looking for life to give me something in return, an equal exchange for what I bring into life, then I'm not attuning to my Gift.

Identity is not transactional. If I take on a self-image or an identity to gain something else, then it's not my core identity and it's most certainly not who I am as a Gift. At a personality level, we may do this often, adjusting our identity to meet the needs, desires, or situations in which we find ourselves; this may be an act of adaptation or even survival. But it is not attuning to one's Gift. Hopefully, this is a helpful clue. On the trail of experiencing one's Gift, the question becomes, who am I when I give myself to life—*not* to meet someone else's needs or expectations but as an expression of who I am as a sacred individual?

Identity

I'm sure the importance I put on knowing our identity is becoming clear. This is true in most areas of our lives, but it is particularly true in working with subtle and spiritual forces and allies. One of the first lessons that my subtle colleague and mentor "John" taught me was to stand in the Light of knowing who I was as a sacred individual when dealing with anything or anyone from the non-physical dimensions of Gaia's ecology.

However, when it came to identity, John meant more than just our soul nature, our Gift, or our Light. He meant the whole of us, soul and personality united in a loving partnership. Our earthly, incarnate self was just as important and vital in the process as our transpersonal and "trans-incarnate" self. John was about transcending all divisions and separations, including the one we can feel between our soul and our personality in order to allow our wholeness to shine.

In the sixties when I began working with John, much was made in the metaphysical and esoteric circles with whom I was familiar about the split between "high self" and "low self," "true self" and "false self," soul and personality. The objective of spiritual practice was to "overcome" or eliminate the latter in order that the former would be in charge.

The idea of bringing greater wholeness and spirit into one's life and behavior, to express according to our "better angels," was laudable, but to split oneself in two to do so was not. "You are a whole system comprised of many parts that need—and want—to work together," John would say, describing what I came to call in Incarnational Spirituality our "incarnational system." "You want to engage with the subtle worlds from the wholeness of who you are, not from one or another of these parts." This was especially true if there was dissension and conflict between the parts.

The story of our human struggle to overcome our baser instincts and the limited vision and behavior of the personality is an old one and defines many dramas of spiritual development. We can be—and are—challenged by the constricted and limited sides of who we are. But the solution is not to cut those sides away but to draw them into the wholeness of who we are, into the Light of our full identity, into the love at the heart of our Gift.

Just as viewing oneself as a Gift can be challenging at times, so loving—or even just liking—and accepting our personality can be challenging at times, too. It may require help, especially if traumatic memories are involved that have damaged our sense of worth. This, however, is beyond the scope of this book. The important point here is simply that we learn to see ourselves as whole persons and value our everyday incarnate identity as much as we may value our spiritual or soul identity, whatever it takes for us to do this. I call this sense of wholeness our incarnate Presence. Attuning to it is the object of the Presence exercise in Incarnational Spirituality, which I outlined earlier in detail in this book.

The Path

With the idea of the Gift and of our whole identity in mind, let's return to the story of co-creating the Gaian Human. On a planetary level, it's a matter of drawing closer together the Stellar Core and the two Sheaths of our collective nature, reducing separation and the influence of the Veils and certainly reducing the effects of the "gunk"—outmoded thought-forms and the persistence of trauma—within them.

On an individual level, something similar is taking place or can take place as a deliberate act of co-creating wholeness. We do so inwardly and in conjunction and collaboration with our Entelechy and with our environment as a whole.

I think of this process as the Path.

Before going further with this story, I want to be clear that the Path can take many forms and applications. There is nothing dogmatic about it. I have a personal approach to it, based on the experiences and understanding I've been sharing with you, but this is certainly not the only way the Path manifests.

The Path is any activity we undertake that seeks, through love, wisdom, intelligence, and will, to bring greater wholeness into ourselves in order to bring greater wholeness into the world. Creating this wholeness is often more than a single person can do on their own, so I see it also as involving cooperation, collaboration, and partnership. Given that it is in service to Gaia as a living being, it is more than a personal psychological enterprise but an engagement with the subtle and spiritual sides of life which is where the fullness of Gaia's presence may be found. Thus, it involves partnership with subtle allies.

Not everyone will feel called to work with subtle allies, and that is fine. They will find their own unique ways of walking this

Path if it calls to them. But to be clear, I am writing this book for those who do feel the call to subtle and spiritual partnerships on behalf of the world. That is the Path I'm on, and it's the one to which I invite you.

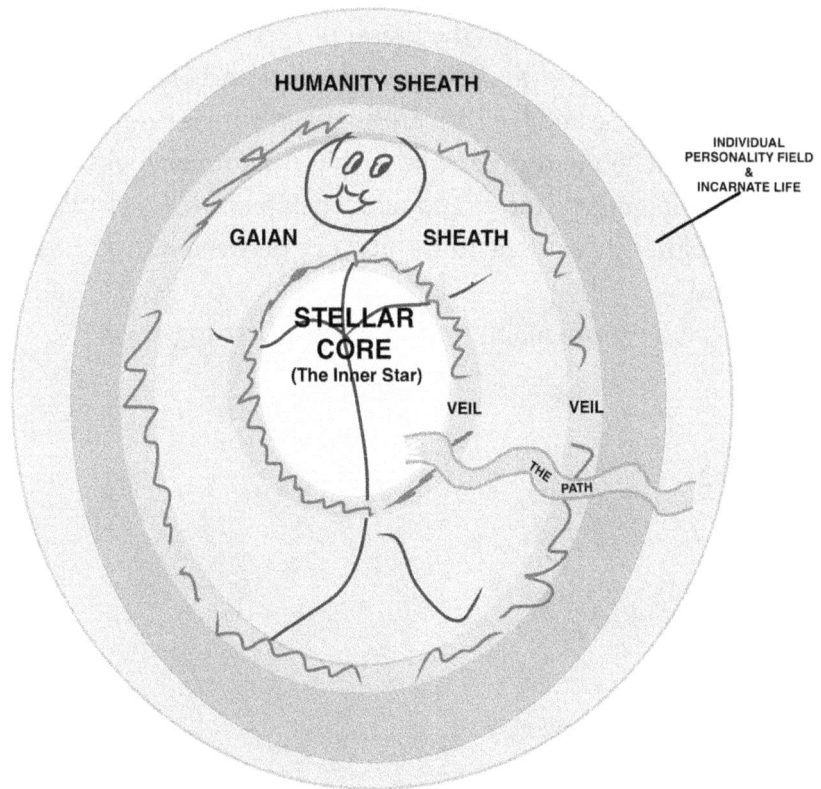

The Path is a connection between our inner Light, our soul's Gift (which ultimately is an expression of the Gift of Cosmic Humanity), and our personality and incarnate life, and through us, with the world. It is a connection that brings together our human nature and our "nature" nature, restoring a sense of animism and the presence of a living earth; in effect, it begins to bridge the separations that have formed between our Gaian and Humanity Sheaths, helping to clear away and heal the psychic and energetic "gunk" that may have accumulated within us. When we do this in partnership with subtle and spiritual allies, this has an effect on the collective unfoldment of the Gaian Human as well.

The Path draws together our personality with our soul's Gift, and in the process, it contributes to uniting into greater wholeness the human and nature parts of who we are.

For those familiar with the Presence exercise in Incarnational Spirituality, there is an interesting correspondence. This is because both this Exercise and the Path are about creating integration and wholeness. The main difference is that the former looks at the unifying, holopoietic forces and relationships within us while the latter explores those same forces at work between ourselves and the world.

Next is a picture mapping the two practices together:

PRESENCE AND PATH COMPARED

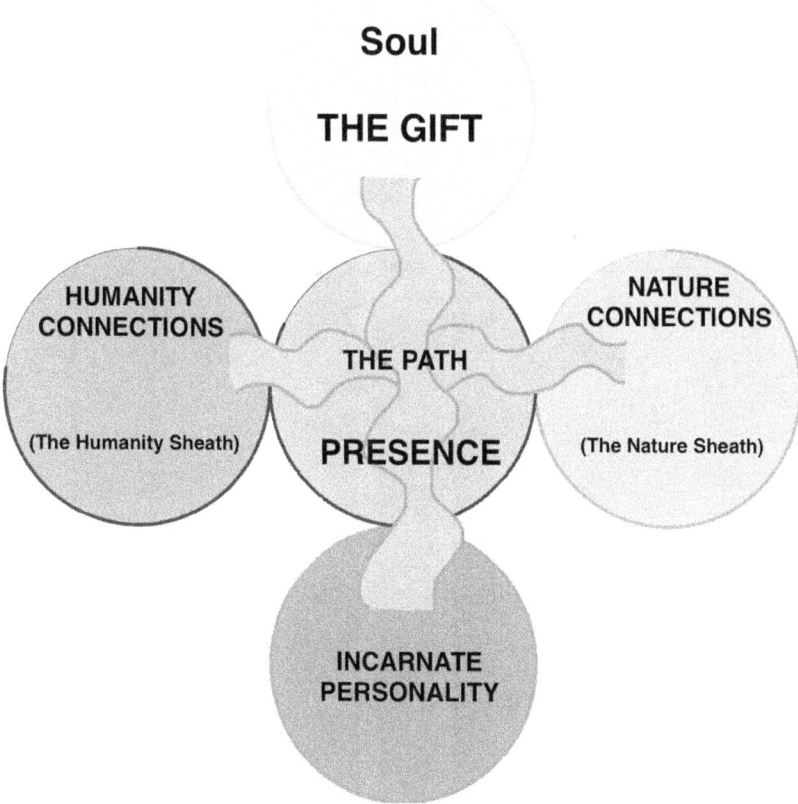

Let's bring this down into a practical experiment. The Path is an act of creating a continuity of connection and love and a flow of wholeness and Light between oneself and the world.

Here is how I practice it:

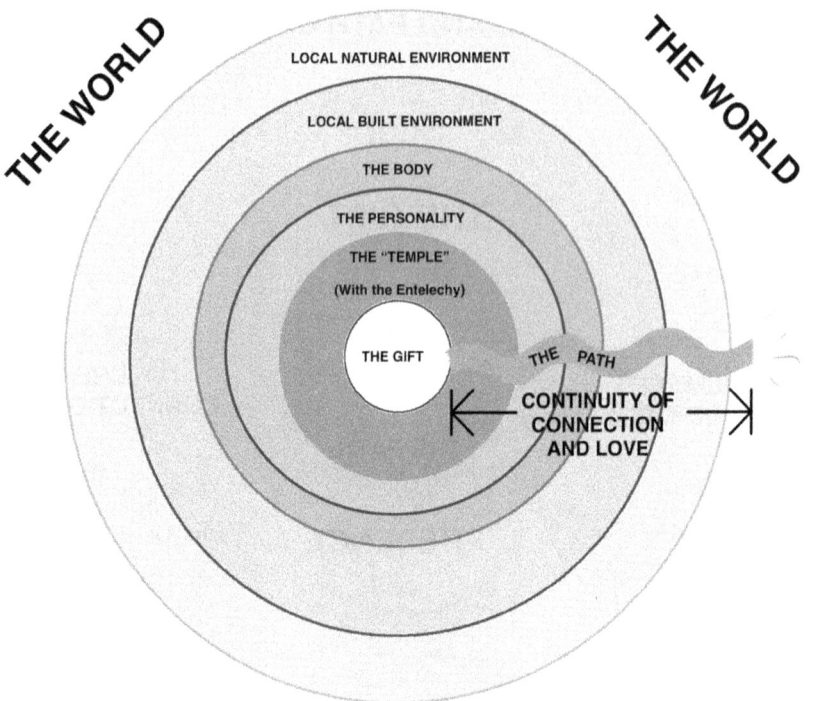

Path of Connection Exercise

- I begin by attuning to my Gift, to the felt sense of sacredness and love, and to its desire and intent to offer itself to the world. This is a wordless, imageless moment of contemplation and attunement. I am just feeling into why I am here in incarnation and the love that lies behind this "why."
- Here I say inwardly, "I am this Gift!"
- Once I have a felt sense of this Presence, this Gift, then I attune to how it manifests as Light (particularly Self-Light) in my life. I think and visualize this as a small inner temple filled with Light, but it could look like anything. It represents a transition from the formlessness of the pure

incarnational intent—the Gift—into a presence of Light: the Gift transforming and offering itself into the realms of form and substance.

- It is at this level that I can draw upon the support and power of my Entelechy. They are, in effect, part of my inner "Temple," part of that which enables my Light to manifest in the world.

- Here I say inwardly, "I am a Presence of Light!"

- Next, I attune to my incarnate self, my personality, seeing it as carrying forward into form and substance the Light from within the "temple," the Light and Love of the Gift. I appreciate and honor my earthly self, knowing it as a part of my wholeness and as a valuable partner in the act of bringing blessing into the world. My personality has strengths and flaws, and it can grow and change, but in the moment, it gives the form necessary for the formless Light to engage the world.

- Here I say inwardly, "My incarnation is a sacred event!"

- Now, I attune to and bless my body with love and appreciation. It is the next step into the world. My body is the partner of my soul, my personality, my Gift, allowing me the privilege and pleasure of engaging the realms of form and substance. It allows me to act in the world.

- Here I say inwardly, "I am grateful for this body and the trillions of lives that make it up. I love that it allows me to be an active part of this world, able to touch, to hear, to see, to taste, to smell, to move. Let love live in and through my body!"

- Moving further outward, I attune to the humanly built world around me, the world of furniture, objects, items, buildings, knick-knacks, tools, appliances, electronics, and so on: the world of my home, the world of human creativity and ingenuity. I bring love and appreciation to the artificial, built things of this world with which I am in touch.

- Here I say inwardly, "I appreciate you and am grateful for what you bring into my life, the comfort and the convenience. I feel the life in you as part of Gaia and bless you with my Light and appreciation. I embrace you with love."

- Then, finally, I attune to the natural environment around me, the earth, the soil, the plants, the animals, the insects: all the natural life of Gaia that lives in my neighborhood and in which I am embedded.

- Here I say inwardly, "I embrace the life and nature around me. I appreciate you and am grateful for what you bring into my life. I bring to you the blessings of Light, the blessings of my Gift."

This sequence of attunements, gratitudes, and blessings is what I use as my Path of connection and continuity between the Gift, the *anwa* of my incarnation, and the world in which I live.

Let's put this into the context of what we've been discussing. An ancient adage has it that "As Above, So Below; as Below, So Above." The microcosm and macrocosm reflect each other, if not exactly then through sympathetic resonance that can create equivalent effects.

On a macrocosmic, planetary level, the veils that have separated Humanity from Nature and from our Stellar Core are thinning, allowing for both a restoration of a forgotten, obscured, or lost unity and the emergence of new, even more dynamic connections. On a microcosmic level, we can do essentially the same thing by uniting the different aspects of our own being into wholeness (which is what the Presence exercise in Incarnational Spirituality is about) and by uniting our wholeness (Soul, Gift, Light, Personality, and Body) with the world around us, both the humanly built world and the world of nature. We are actively bringing love, gratefulness, and appreciation into each of these levels, and bringing them into deeper connection with each other.

This is a magical act of resonance, one in which anyone can participate, drawing our everyday humanity together with the Light and spirit of the Cosmos in a holopoietic, Gaian-healing partnership.

If my understanding is correct and new cosmic energies of Light are indeed becoming a part of the overall ecology and metabolism of the Earth, it is our Stellar Core—the part of each of us and all of us that remains part of Cosmic Humanity—that can most easily relate to and assimilate these new energies. This may be true, but this Stellar Core can seem abstract or distant, a metaphysical or mystical idea that has little bearing on our everyday incarnate life.

This is only true if we allow it to be true and do nothing to translate the idea of the Stellar Core and the Gift it represents into practice and action. The Path, or some equivalent process of connection and continuity, is an example of such a practice. The Stellar Core of our being is not some distant spiritual presence. It is part of our wholeness, part of who we are, whether we are conscious of it or not. When we deliberately invoke this part of our wholeness, as when we attune to our Gift and draw its Light and love into all aspects of our life and world through something like the Path, then we are turning what is unconscious into a conscious flow of energy and presence.

When we practice our wholeness and stand in our sacred

identity, we are deliberately and mindfully building the unity that allows the Gaian Human—and a healing Gaia—to emerge.

We do not have to do this alone. We have help. We have allies, if we are also willing to be allies. Which brings us to the Gaian Alliance.

PART VI: THE GAIAN ALLIANCE

Three Zones

In my inner journeys into the subtle worlds, I have the experience of crossing energetic thresholds. When I do so, the whole feel of the subtle environment around me changes, and the way in which beings present themselves and communicate changes as well. Whether others experience this phenomenon, I don't know, but it has been a prominent feature of my own engagement with Gaia's subtle ecology.

It reminds me of driving to Canada, which is a three-hour drive north of where I live. If not for the Customs checkpoints, the actual boundary along the land would be invisible, but you would know you've crossed a border because the feel of Canada is different from that of the United States. Suddenly all the road signs give distances in kilometers instead of miles, and gasoline is sold in liters and not gallons.

As a result of this experience, I postulate the existence of three broad, different "zones" in the subtle worlds. If I were describing a physical ecology, I would probably call these zones *bioregions*. Since I'm describing what essentially are areas of consciousness, I could perhaps call them *noöregions* after *nous*, the Greek word for *mind*. This is the same construction the Jesuit philosopher, paleontologist and geologist, Teilhard de Chardin, used when he called the field of human thought enveloping the globe, the *noösphere*.

Over the years, I have experienced many "subzones" and divisions within each of these three great *noöregions* and lots of differentiation between beings depending on the subzone they were from, but still the experience of these three major regions is paramount. This experience of crossing these major thresholds came to profoundly shape my "map" or sense of the subtle worlds.

I call these three zones or *noöregions* the *Subtle Environment*, the *Subtle Worlds*, and the *Spiritual Worlds*. The boundaries between these three zones are not hard; they are fluid and permeable, with one zone flowing into the other.

The *Subtle Environment* (which includes what in esoteric lore is known as the *etheric* dimension) is in many ways a reflection of the physical world. It is filled with subtle energies that directly relate to or are influenced and shaped by life in the physical domain. Such subtle energies are themselves sentient and living, though not "beings" in the sense of possessing consciousness or self-awareness; they represent the main currents of nurturing and vitalizing energies that help support the health and wholeness of physical manifestations. They are a vital part of Gaia's energy metabolism. Thus, looking out my window at the fir trees standing in my front yard, the subtle environment would contain the etheric or subtle fields of living energy surrounding each tree as well as energies of vitality that flow between them or to them from higher frequencies of spiritual life. For a more detailed discussion of the subtle environment, please see my book *Working With Subtle Energies.*

The *Subtle Worlds,* on the other hand, are realms in which life and consciousness manifest as "energy systems" or "energy forms." These subtle energies are not physical energies such as heat or electricity. "Energy" in this context is a form of matter vibrating at a higher frequency than physical matter and possessing greater fluidity of form and substance than the latter. One could say that these are realms in which form and consciousness are one and the same, rather than form being an instrument through which consciousness is expressed.

Some domains within the subtle worlds (and the beings for whom those domains are their home) work to sustain and empower the physical world, providing the vital energies and blessings that manifest within the subtle environment. Other domains and their inhabitants function to serve or express aspects of Gaia, the World Soul, that have little or nothing to do with the physical world but instead may offer unique opportunities for growth and learning just as the physical dimension does. Still, other domains in the subtle worlds may be in relationship to solar and cosmic energies coming from the universal environment that Gaia itself occupies. Some of the subtle realms are well within the reach and scope of human thought while others are beyond our imagination.

Generally speaking, the subtle worlds are the realms of beings who manifest through various kinds of energy forms.

The *Spiritual Worlds* transcend the energy manifestations of the subtle realms and manifest as pure spirit and presence. These are the realms of the soul. Whereas beings and forces in the subtle worlds work with the energy aspects of planetary life, the spiritual realms work with the forces and qualities of sacredness and soul within all things. They nurture and express the Gifts at the heart of all manifestation. These are the realms of many of the angelic and Devic forces that overlight the incarnation of sacredness within the realms of matter and energy. These are the realms of Beings who manifest through various frequencies of Light, which in this context is not a subtle energy. Here's a picture:

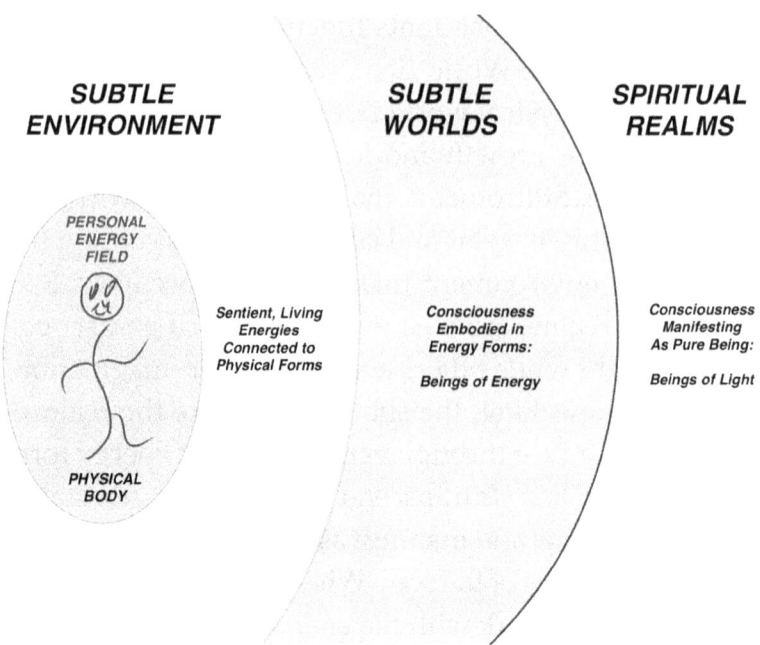

Equally important is understanding that we occupy the same three zones during our incarnational sojourn in the physical world. We are obviously in a physical body, but we each possess bodies or fields of energy and Light that correspond and correlate to the subtle environment around us, the greater ecology of the subtle worlds, and the spiritual realms beyond.

I show this in the following picture:

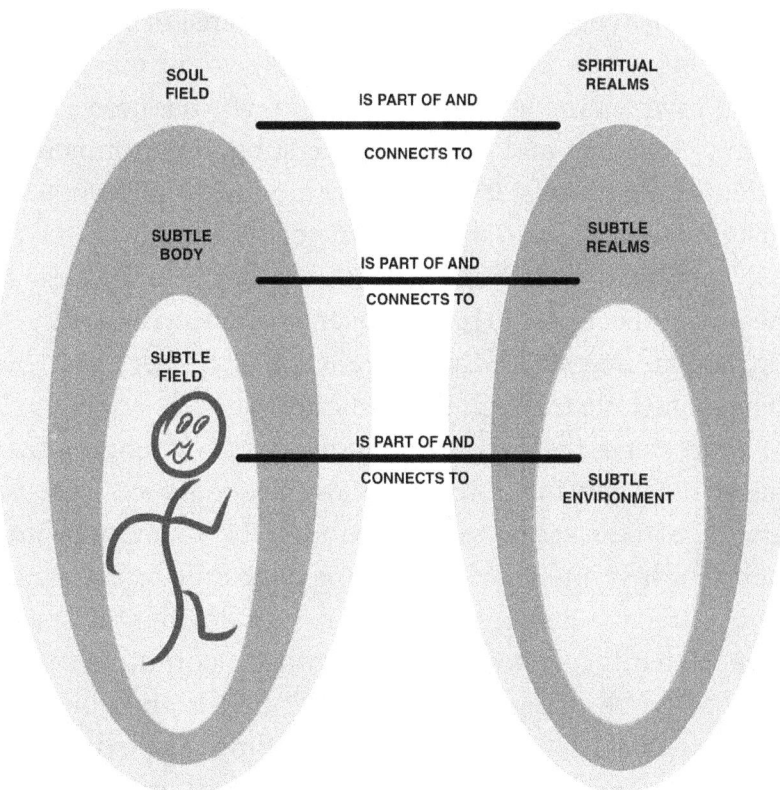

It's because we are individuals with both spiritual and subtle bodies that I talk about engaging with the subtle and spiritual energies and beings. It is an acknowledgment of the existence of these "zones" of expression and manifestation.

Modes of Connection

We are each a subtle and spiritual energy ecosystem in engagement with the subtle and spiritual ecosystems of a planetary Spirit, Gaia. This means that when it comes to forming connections, there are different ways in which this can happen. Here are some examples from my own experience.

On rare occasions, I have been in touch with two

individuals working from the etheric dimension close to the energy field of the physical world. One is a young man, Lewis, who was killed in the Vietnam War and who has held a focus of consciousness and energy in the subtle environment in order to better minister to incarnate individuals. The other is a woman who died in the late Nineteenth Century but who also chooses to hold her consciousness and energy close to the physical in order to be of greater assistance. Both of these individuals may well be able to function on higher levels, but they contact me through their etheric forms.

I experience them as distinct individuals who engage with me telepathically in an ordinary conversational way. They use language in the same way I do, though the meaning behind their words is often enriched by the telepathic connection.

In effect, we share a familiar, human mental space. Paradoxically, this can both facilitate communication because we're using words together and limit it because words themselves are limited and limiting. The experience for me is one of being a separate individual engaged with other individuals different and separate from myself, not altogether different from an ordinary conversation with another incarnate person.

I have had this experience, though more rarely, with beings in the subtle environment who are not human but who have a history of experience of engagement with human beings and thus are familiar and comfortable using words and language telepathically.

As a second example, I work, almost on a daily basis, with a small group of beings, both human and non-human, that operate in the subtle world rather than in the subtle environment. I call them my "subtle colleagues." Invariably, we connect not through my mind or psyche telepathically but through direct interaction between my subtle body and theirs. Our fields blend in what I call a *collaborative mind*, a topic I'll discuss in more detail later in this book.

In this state, I still experience myself as David Spangler, a unique individuality, but I also experience myself as a participant in a collective consciousness, a small "group mind" that involves myself and whichever of my subtle colleagues are taking part in that moment.

What passes between us is challenging to describe. It is a blend of feeling, thought, images, and impressions, but in fact, meaning is transmitted through a resonance of energy. The energy we share between us is itself the form of communication, and it can be richly packed with meaning, so much so that it can take me hours, days, even months to fully unpack, translate, and assimilate what was transmitted in a matter of seconds.

When words are exchanged in conversation, they can change our minds and our feelings, but we remain fundamentally unchanged. When subtle energy is exchanged, our subtle bodies change in some manner. I come away from these encounters of collaborative mind not quite the same person energetically or structurally as I was when the conversation began.

Then there are beings operating out of the Spiritual Zone. My first subtle mentor, "John," was one of these, though he could also communicate subtle energy to subtle energy. I think of communication at this level as "soul touch." Again, there is a blending of beingness and consciousness, and out of this blending, this soul touch, meaning unfolds and blossoms in my own being, as if it had always been there. Although I can be aware that I am in contact with a distinct consciousness from my own, there is no overriding sense of separation that would turn us into two different people. We become one, with no loss of our unique identities but rather an expansion into a shared identity—or into a world of shared meaning.

Like subtle energy communication, this soul touch can bring into being within me a rich eruption of meaning that may then take me hours, days, or even months to fully assimilate and understand; or understanding may come in an instant and I am transformed by it.

I illustrate these three modes of contact and communication in the following picture:

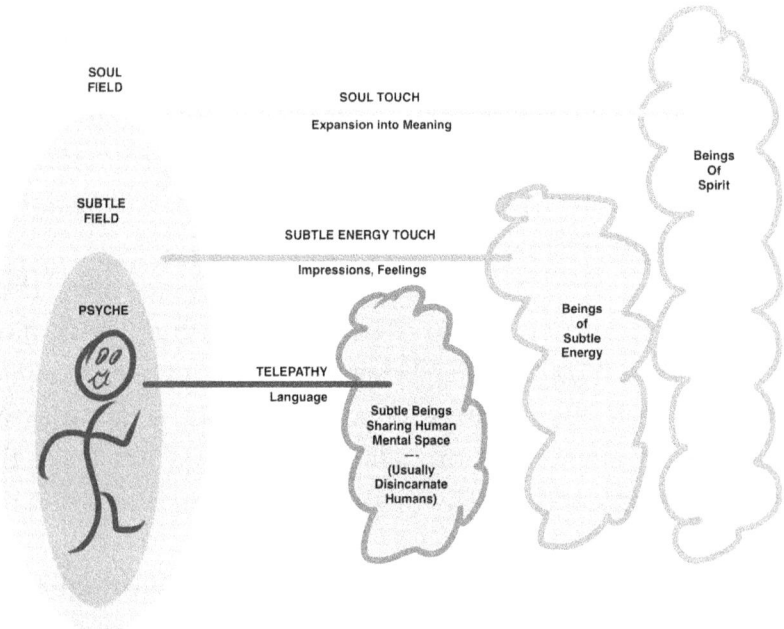

This is not the whole picture of contact, however. The three "zones" are embedded in and are part of Gaia as a whole. When we contact any subtle or spiritual being, we are implicitly (and at times explicitly) also in contact with the whole of Gaia's metabolism, ecology, and life.

Eco-Contact

This brings up a part of my experience in contacting the

subtle and spiritual realms that I have rarely, if ever, seen written or spoken about, and that is the ecological dimension of such contacts.

I think the main reason is that we are conditioned to think in terms of separate individualities, our own and those of the things around us. We forget the ecological truism that all organisms are coupled with their environment and that the nature of the organism is shaped to some degree by the local ecosystem. Instead, we "de-couple" everything, especially ourselves, from the environments around us. It's not surprising, then, that when we encounter a subtle or spiritual phenomenon or being, we usually see it and deal with it as if it were something isolated and separate in itself.

The actual picture looks something more like this:

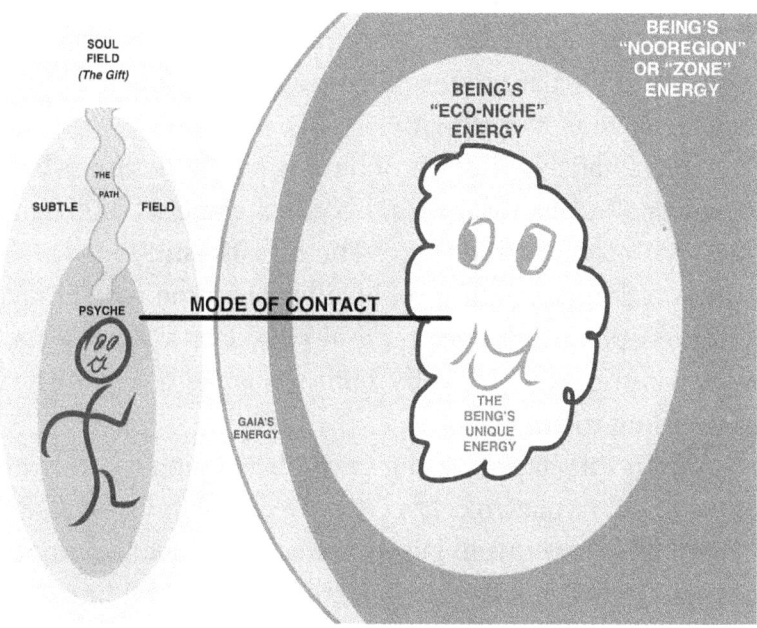

In principle, then, when we are in contact with a subtle or spiritual being, we are in contact with its unique energy field but also with the energy field and characteristics of its native environment or "eco-niche," the energy field of the zone in which it is operating (subtle environment, subtle realms, or spiritual realms), and with the overall energy field of Gaia.

On a practical level, does this mean that anytime I connect in partnership with a subtle or spiritual ally, I will have to deal with four different levels and qualities of energy? No, at least not in my experience. However, implicitly, all four are present (and perhaps others as well—subtle organisms, being multi-dimensional, are not always bound to or present in a single environment the way a physical organism or person is) and can exert an influence.

But one way this does manifest is that the overall energy field of a subtle or spiritual entity can be more impactful than either you (or I) or the being involved expected. This can be especially true of a non-human being, such as a nature spirit, Deva, or an angel, who is not familiar with human beings or experienced at moderating and modulating their overall energy to match our own.

I have had experiences of having my "inner fuses blown" because a subtle or spiritual contact came in too hard, too fast, with too much energy. The usual result is that I "shut down" etherically and psychically for a time, and I may feel fatigued physically, effects that only last a short time and which can be alleviated by taking a walk, a nap, or having something to eat.

When this happens, the immediate thing to do is to ask the contact to back off. It's why we can always say "No!" to any subtle or spiritual being, especially if we feel unable to integrate the energies they are presenting at that time. If it is a good and honest contact, one seeking only our best interests, then they will back off, perhaps to recalibrate and try again later. After all, the point is to form a partnership, not to blow us away with their power!

There is something else important that we can do, something that we've been discussing right along. The more we bring unity and wholeness into our own personal energy field, through a practice like the Path, the more we resonate with the wholeness of Gaia, with all its zones and all its ecosystems. It's in finding our wholeness through love that we gain the capacity to encounter, engage with, and integrate the diversity of Gaia.

Collaborative Mind

The nature of the energy relationship and exchange between ourselves and a subtle or spiritual being is an important consideration in the creation of what I experience as a "collaborative mind" or "collaborative field." This is a state in which thoughts, images, ideas, and insights can flow between two or more participants as if they were sharing a single, coordinated mind, one in which new insights can emerge beyond what any of the participants could generate on their own. There's no loss of individuality within such a field but there is communion and a sense of participating in a larger field of mind and awareness.

This is the relationship I usually have with my subtle colleagues.

When people think of partnerships, they likely think of an arrangement between two or more people that is transactional, that is, as a relationship of exchange between the parties involved who otherwise remain separate. Where a relationship with a subtle or spiritual being is concerned, this exchange might be that of ideas, guidance, information, wisdom, prophecy, and so on, or it may be more energetic in nature, an exchange of qualities.

Certainly, transactional relationships do form and exist between incarnate people and subtle and spiritual beings, and they can be for the benefit of all concerned, as when people worship or give offerings to a spiritual being who in turn blesses them and their endeavors. At times, such transactions can be to the detriment of one or another party. Folk tales are full of accounts of people who sell their souls to the Devil in exchange for some temporary earthly benefit.

A collaborative mind or field, however, is not transactional. It is synergic, one in which a larger field emerges in the moment that is greater than the sum of its parts but a field that also honors and empowers the individual parts.

For such a synergic, collaborative field to come into being, there needs to be an equivalency of energy between all the participants. Their energy contribution to this whole need not be equal or the same, but if I'm creating a collaborative mind with a subtle or spiritual being, then what I bring to the table, energetically speaking, needs to match and blend what they bring. If they—or I—bring either too much energy or too little, this blending doesn't take place. There is an imbalance that keeps the participants apart and turns the potential partnership into something more transactional than collaborative. There can still be a useful exchange, but the flow of life, information, love, and qualities between the participants will not be as deep, holistic, and emergent as it could be.

There is a way of creating this energy equivalency. I call it *Alliance Space*.

Alliance Space

Alliance Space is a psychological and energetic tool that we'll use in forming the Gaian-oriented partnerships we'll explore in the rest of this book. I first learned it from my subtle colleague and mentor, "John." Here's an illustration of what's involved:

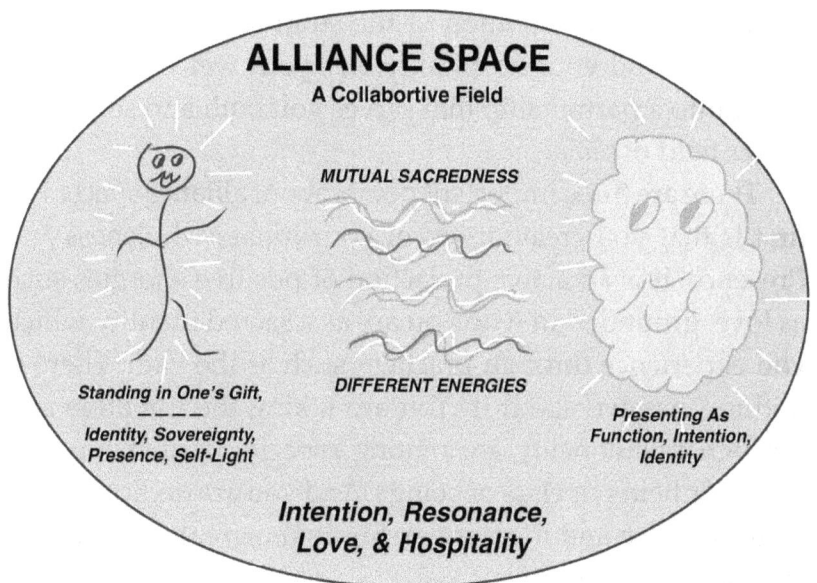

This may look complex, but it's really very simple. It draws on everything we've been talking about and puts it together as an act of connection.

Let's break it down.

When you engage with a subtle or spiritual being, the energy will be different between you, but you share a mutual sacredness. It is this sacredness that connects you and which can moderate and blend the energies between you to create a collaborative field, an "alliance space."

For the subtle or spiritual being in question, its sacredness manifests through its function, its intention or Gift, and its identity. We'll see examples of this as we proceed. For you, sacredness manifests as you stand in your Gift, standing in the integrity of your identity, your Sovereignty, Presence, and Self-Light.

The actual alliance space is a field of energy that you offer toward a specific subtle or spiritual being. It is based on your intention to connect, your ability to come into resonance with the function and intention of the subtle or spiritual being, your love, and your hospitality, i.e., your welcoming of the being into a partnership that serves you both and serves the larger field of Gaia.

There are three important points about alliance space. The first is that you create it out of your innate wholeness and Presence; it is an active projection of positive energies such as love, grounded in who you are as a sacred identity which you experience through practices such as the Path. There is nothing passive about it. You are taking the initiative and through intentionality, are inviting a specific partnership with a specific being or class of beings. And you are dedicating the alliance space and the partnership to the greater wholeness and well-being of Gaia.

Secondly, alliance space creates an energy boundary based on that dedication and intent and resonates with your positive energies. For this reason, it also functions as a field of protection and discernment against any toxic or malicious energies that might be in the environment. You are not invoking such energies, and they cannot abide by the Light generated by your alliance space.

In effect, creating alliance space can have the effect of altering the local subtle energy environment towards wholeness and Light. Remember that organisms in an ecosystem are coupled with their environment. Change the latter, and you change the nature of the subtle organisms and living energies that can make that environment their home.

The third important element is that alliance space is a coming together of a shared intent and an enhancement of function. In other words, you are saying to a potential partner, "Let me draw on my spiritual resources in order to help you do the work you are trying to do."

Take, for example, the Deva of a maple tree. The intent

and function of that Deva is to bring blessing and vitality to the life and growth of that tree. When you form an alliance space with that Deva, you are specifically aligning with that intent and with that function. You are bringing your own Light, your own love, your own subtle and spiritual energies into a partnership to help the Deva bless and energize the maple tree.

It is quite possible that something more may happen, that in the partnership you form something new emerges from the synergy of both you and your ally, something unexpected and more powerful than either of you could do on your own. If so, that is icing on the cake.

It will be seen here that alliance space is, to use our earlier metaphors, a "metabolic" function. The metabolism of Gaia is such that energies are generated and flow along networks of relationships between various subtle and spiritual beings. We are all part of Gaia's living circulatory energy system. Alliance space is a deliberate enhancement of this process, creating a partnership of intention and function that expands this circulation from one level of life to another.

This is a general overview of alliance space. We'll see it used specifically as we follow the Path of Contact for the remainder of this book.

The Path of Contact

At this point, we are going to apply everything you've been learning in this book. We are going to use the by-now-familiar metaphor of the Path, but rather than moving from the Gift and Soul outward into our life and world, we are going to start with the subtle realm closest to us and work our way outward into more energetic, complex, and planetary regions of Gaia's ecology and the beings who inhabit them.

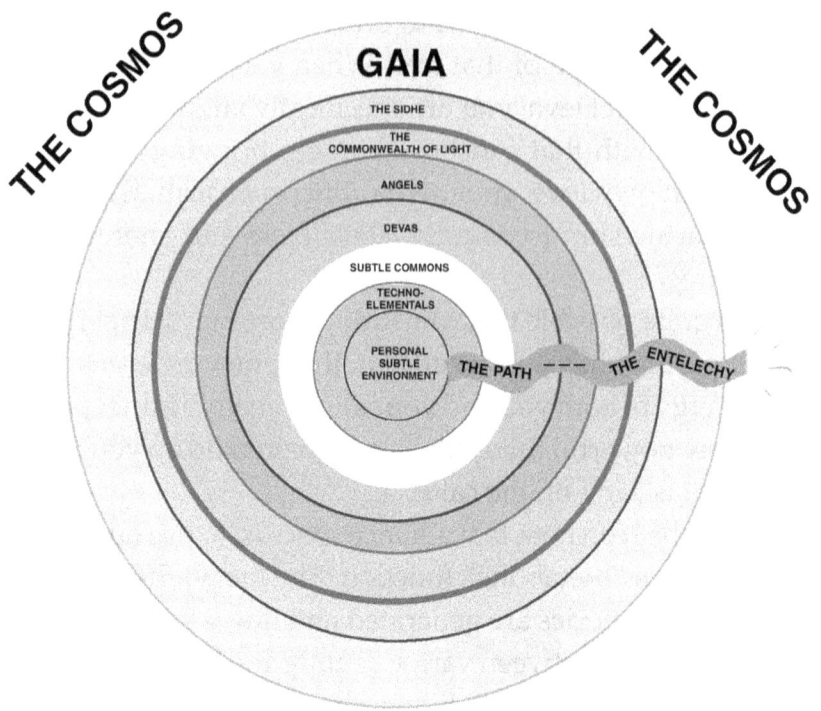

Please note again the image of the "Path" as a process, an act of continuity and connection, contributing to the release and expression of a holopoietic energy. Also, as we move through each of these levels, we are always accompanied by our Entelechy, the field of support generated by our natural allies. The idea of the Path and the presence of the Entelechy provide a unifying element throughout our engagements with the greater subtle and spiritual worlds.

As we start, let's review our objectives here. Gaia is going through what we may symbolize as a cosmic initiation, taking on new energies from its stellar environment. This in turn requires a clearing, a healing, and an expansion of Gaia's own internal energy ecosystems and metabolism in order to handle these newer energies. Humanity's own collective energy systems (not to mention our individual ones) are also needing to respond and adapt accordingly—all of which are creating challenge and difficulty at a physical level.

All subtle and spiritual energies are mediated through living beings, through their consciousnesses and energy fields. Therefore, there are subtle and spiritual beings operating at many levels of Gaia's life and metabolism, but particularly at those levels in direct reception of the cosmic energies that are taking on and processing these new energies, "digesting" them, so to speak, assimilating them, and making them available to others through networking and partnership. We, as incarnate humans, are invited to join this process.

The key lies in forming partnerships that are dedicated to serving Gaia, thereby building the chains of resonance that will sound the note of wholeness throughout the Gaian metabolism, breaking up old resistances and obstructions, and clearing space for the newer life to emerge.

It's through these partnerships that we walk the Path of Contact as Gaian Humans, creating a Gaian Alliance that brings wholeness into our lives and into our world.

The Personal Subtle Environment

The most immediate and generally the most accessible subtle environment is the one that surrounds each of us in our everyday lives, homes, and workplaces.

In our bodies, the majority of cells, those that are not part of the bloodstream, are surrounded by interstitial fluid. This fluid bathes the cells, bringing them food and energy and removing cellular waste. It forms the immediate environment of the cell.

In the living organism that is Gaia, the subtle environment is the energy equivalent of the interstitial fluid. It is an energy "atmosphere," the subtle "air" or fluid around us. The subtle energies it contains surround us and determine the overall character of our subtle environment. Are these energies basically positive or negative?

The subtle environment is a complex, multi-layered planetary field that is the immediate contact point through which subtle and spiritual energies from the higher dimensions reach into the physical world. Think of sunlight reaching the earth through our planet's atmosphere. If the sky is clear, the land basks in the warmth of the sun. If the sky is cloudy or smoggy, much less sunlight makes it through. A similar phenomenon occurs with the subtle environment, but it can be very localized.

In my physical neighborhood, if the sky is clear, it's clear for every house. If the air is filled with smoke from distant forest fires, smoky pollution is there for every house. But the subtle environment is more nuanced. It is responsive to the energies of thought and feeling being generated by different people in different places.

For instance, in one household, a family may make a daily practice of blessing the subtle environment of their home, filling it with love. The family next door, however, may be mired in domestic difficulties, filling their subtle environment with angry and fearful energies. In the former case, Light can easily shine into that household from higher levels; the "sky" is clear, so to speak. In the latter, much less Light penetrates the clouds of negative emotions that have gathered and allowed to settle in that particular environment. A matter of just a few physical feet may separate one household from another, and yet, the subtle environment of each is vastly different, with different consequences for those living within them.

These boundaries or energy differentials are not "hard," like a wall. A home in a neighborhood can have an energy influence beyond its property line or its structure, depending on the situation. That loving household may generate an energy field of friendliness and tolerance that fills the entire neighborhood with goodwill. The opposite is also true, that the hate-filled house may spread its negativity beyond its walls. Much depends on what others are doing and how others are responding. There are other variables as well, for human beings are not the only species that influences the quality of the subtle environment. The presence of land that has been damaged or an ecosystem that has been disrupted can also generate negative energies within the local subtle environment. The reverse is true when an effort is made to honor the land and restore its ecological balance.

Though the quality of a particular subtle environment can be localized and dependent upon or shaped by what is happening in its corresponding physical environment, there can be planetary effects as well. When the Trade Towers were attacked and fell on September 11, 2001, a wave of fear swept through many of the subtle environments of America and subsequently of the world. This was partly due to the reactions of the people living in those environments as they responded emotionally and mentally to the news of the attacks, but there was also a wave of fearful energy that swept through the "interstitial fluid" of Gaia that was collective in nature.

Likewise, a positive event, especially one that captures the imagination of people around the world (think of a Taylor Swift concert, for instance), can generate a wave of goodwill that can spread far beyond its immediate local origin. This is because, from a planetary perspective, there is only one subtle environment, just as there is only one planetary atmosphere, even though it may manifest through different forms of weather in different places.

The boundaries of any particular subtle environment are

variable and permeable, depending on the situation. The subtle environment of my house, for example, is bounded and defined by the walls of my home, whereas the subtle environment of my front lawn is open to the flow of subtle energies within the neighborhood (though it may still be defined in part by the particular trees, flowers, shrubs, bushes, rocks, and so forth that make up our yard's particular landscaping).

Speaking generally, then, we may say that any given subtle environment has two primary characteristics: the subtle energy emanations arising from whatever the physical characteristics (and in our case, the mental and emotional characteristics) are within that environment, and the currents or flows of subtle energies that move through that environment from other sources.

For instance, I live in a valley surrounded by the foothills of the Cascade Mountain Range, with the Olympic Mountain Range on the horizon to the west. When I sit in my front yard, I can feel the subtle energies arising from our lawn, from the fir trees that border our property, from the boulders that surround the lawn, and the different flowers my wife and daughter have planted. It's a cozy energy, and one filled with life.

At the same time, especially at certain times of the day such as early morning, I can feel the transmissions of vital subtle energies flowing out and down from the surrounding mountains, bringing with them the blessings of the mountain Devas (about which I shall write more in a moment). These energies move like a wave through the neighborhood, their qualities being absorbed by the soil, the plants, and the animal life. I find this flow invigorating and uplifting as if I have been touched by the spaciousness and purity of the mountain peaks.

This subtle environment has an intelligence and a function of its own, which is to reflect and hold all the living energies of the things within an environment in a nourishing field of energy AND to provide a conduit for higher energies of Light to touch the earth and be assimilated within the physical (and in our case, psychological, mental, and emotional) dimensions. It is the "interstitial fluid" of Gaia.

I think of it this way: the subtle environment is like a cloud that brings moisture to the land, but how much of this moisture will the land absorb? How closely can the "cloud" connect with the "land?" The fact is, there are several factors, especially within the human world, that can interfere with or block the "moisture," the energies of Light and blessing. Our own negative projections, both personal and collective as a species, can do so. The shape of our buildings, how they are constructed, the materials within them, their orientation to lines of magnetism and energy flow within the body of the earth (the fabled *ley lines*), the uses to which they are put, and how regularly, if at all, they are energetically cleansed: all these things can affect how Light can pass through a particular subtle environment and into the physical world that it embraces and contains.

Many years ago, I was invited to give a workshop at a retreat center on the East Coast. The event started off well, but as we went on, I began to feel that I was wading through molasses, something sticky and resistant to the energy work we were doing. Finally, it came time for a lunch break, and everyone left the room to eat. Alone, I then did an inner scan of the room, something I should have done at the very beginning, and discovered pockets of stale, negative energies attached to the walls, the floor, and even the large pillows that some people had been using to sit or lie upon. I then proceeded to do a thorough subtle energy cleansing of the room, something I think of as "energy hygiene." When people came back from lunch, the room felt energetically clear, and we had no further trouble doing our work that afternoon.

Later, talking to one of the people who ran the center, I commented on my experience. She explained that the room we had been using was one several other teachers used for primal scream and other cathartic workshops, encouraging people to release all their pent-up negative feelings, pounding the pillows, yelling, and so forth. That served those people, but no one was performing any energy hygiene afterward. All that negative outpouring, all this "dandruff," was allowed to build up, like subtle cobwebs and dust bunnies, collecting and making the subtle environment of that room stale and resistant to positive energies.

By contrast, I have been in rooms, even in old, otherwise dilapidated buildings, where the occupants have paid attention to the subtle environment, doing their best to make it positive, clean, clear, and resonant with the Light.

Whether it is simple or complex in its manifestation, we may not think of partnering with the subtle environment any more than we usually think of partnering with the air around us. But all subtle energies are alive and sentient; for this reason, our local subtle environment may not be a "being", but it is a presence. It is responsive to the energy with which we engage it.

What does it mean, then, to form alliance space with my local subtle environment? How do I do so, and why? Let me use the subtle environment of my living room—which is where I am writing this on my iPad—as an example.

While our house as a whole has its own energy feel to it, every room in our house also has a different subtle energy field (and feel) to it, depending on its usage, who spends time in it, and so on. One of the exercises I would give to participants in my subtle energy classes would be to walk from one room in their home to another, paying attention to how the felt sense of the energy (the subtle environment) would change as they crossed the threshold into a new room. (If you would like to read more about this, my friend and Lorian colleague, Timothy Hass, has written two wonderful books on the topic: *The Wonder-Full World of the Home* and *The Wonder-Full World of the Home: The Second Story.*)

Our living room is perfectly ordinary: a couple of sofas, two chairs, some end tables, lamps, a coffee table, a television, and there is also a fireplace. It's where, as a family, we spend a great deal of time, and where we entertain visitors and guests. It's where I do most of my writing these days, as well, with my iPad on my lap as I sit in "Dad's chair." So, it's a happily lived-in space, and its subtle environment reflects that.

I do not have to be outdoors on our lawn or in our backyard to attune to the flows and currents of subtle energy that move through our neighborhood, either from the foothills or mountains around or from nearby Lake Sammamish, a large lake that is a prominent feature of the valley in which I live. If I pay attention and attune to them, I can draw those larger flows into the house and into the living room, where they can bless the things around me in the house. The walls of the house do not need to pose a barrier to such flows, but I need to be the conduit or the connection that opens the interior of the home to them (just as I might need to open a window to let in a fresh breeze from outside, airing out the house).

In this instance, I want to form an alliance space with the subtle energies in my living room in order to align and attune with the Light and the newer energies flowing into Gaia. I want to do this because the subtle environment is the "landing place" for such energies as they move from the cosmic and stellar dimensions into resonance with and assimilation by the physical world. In effect, I want to draw these energies down to earth, in partnership with my immediate, local subtle environment—in this case, that of my living room.

Remember, alliance space is an energy field of intention, love, and resonance, grounded in our Path, our sense of our incarnational Gift, our sense of sacred identity. It is a particular kind of invitational sharing of oneself in service to a task or a function.

My first step, then, is to stand in my sacredness, my *anwa*, my Gift, and honor the Path of Blessing and incarnation that connects my sacred core, my Stellar Core, with my soul, my subtle energy, my personality, and my body.

I acknowledge this as my identity.

I acknowledge this as the source of the love I now bring to the act of creating an alliance with the subtle environment here in my living room and its function of bringing Light into the physical environment around me. Please note that if I have been practicing this—practicing the Path or its equivalent—this process of shifting into this identity can be almost instantaneous.

My intent in alliance space is to resonate with the function of the subtle environment as part of Gaia's metabolism and circulatory system. I want to add my subtle and spiritual energy to that of the Intelligence at work within the subtle environment to enhance this function, to enable it to bring even more "moisture" than usual to the physical "land" of my living room and all within it. I am linking my sacredness with the inherent sacredness within the subtle environment itself. It is also possible to involve my Entelechy in this process, adding the energy and Light of this supportive field to the creation of this alliance space.

Ordinarily, whether I call upon my Entelechy or not, this might be all I need to do. I am taking a moment to form an alliance with a subtle and spiritual presence in order to increase the flow of blessing in and through that presence to the room around me. Partnering in this way, we have synergy, creating a whole that is more than the sum of its parts. The Light moving within the subtle environment increases, the Light within me increases, the Light within the room increases. Blessings all around.

I can do this kind of simple alliance space anytime I wish, and in fact, it is a regular part of my daily practice. If nothing else, it is a powerful act of energy hygiene, and it gives me a wonderful sense of partnering with the life of the world.

However, in the context of this book, I am after something else, something more.

Here is where my ability to touch my Gift, my Stellar Core, is important and is developed through practice. It is this part of me that is a remnant or a continuation of my soul's ancient origin in Cosmic Humanity, a living memory of being one with the Stellar Realms, that is already resonant with the new energies entering the earth and becoming part of Gaia. It may not know these new energies specifically, but it is familiar with the stellar vibration and what it takes to anchor it into form and matter, because it has done so as part of humanity's evolutionary journey and because it is doing so now through the layers and complexity of my incarnation.

It recognizes a family vibe.

So, using the Path or its equivalent practice, I draw myself into a wholeness touched by this Stellar Core, this ancient and ever-present Gift manifested through uncounted Incarnational Gifts. I am this identity, and I offer the resonance of this identity to the Intelligence of the subtle environment of my living room in partnership to enhance its ability and capacity to touch and draw down into contact with the physical plane the new stellar and cosmic energies coursing through Gaia.

When I do this, I feel more than just an enhancement of a spiritual Light becoming part of the subtle environment of the living room and thus part of the energy fields and lives of everything within the physical living room. It's difficult to describe, but it's a feeling of renewal, of something new becoming part of the world, something spacious and freeing and filled with love. It feels like the pure Light of a star enters my living room.

It's an inadequate description, but it's the best I can do. Science tells us that everything in the world ultimately comes from "star stuff," born from the nuclear heart of stars. In this moment of alliance space, as the star in me connects in loving partnership with the star within the subtle environment, it's as if everything in the room remembers its origin and for a moment, reveals and celebrates its own inner star.

I stay in this state as long as is comfortable. It need not be a long time. When I feel finished, I give thanks to my partner, my ally of the subtle environment, and release it from the alliance space. Basically, I allow this space to collapse around me, allowing each of us to continue on our own way, having shared a moment of blessing together.

I always end by reaffirming my Sovereignty, my Presence, my Self-Light, my Gift.

The fact is, given the nature of subtle phenomena and the fact that each of us is a unique "platform" for sensing such phenomena, what you and I experience in a case like this may well be different. Hence, what is there for me might take a different form for you. I do not offer recipes that must be followed; I offer examples of what might be. You will need to practice and explore to discover what it is for you.

Techno-Elementals

One of my earliest experiences as a child was perceiving that all the things in our household were alive in some mysterious way. They held and projected a living energy. Thus, for me, the sofa was alive, the chairs were alive, the dining room table was alive, and so forth. I have a vivid memory of going to a movie with my parents when I was six or so which featured a Disney cartoon to start with. In this cartoon, all the furniture in a house came alive and was conversing and interacting with the main character. I remember thinking with amazement, "They've made a movie about my world!"

Of course, in my world, the furniture didn't get up under its own will and move about or talk to me. I certainly knew the difference between our sofa and our cat! But I could feel the energy field within and around the sofa, I could project love to it, and I could feel its response. At some level of life and beingness that I could experience but not understand, there was sentiency there. I was surrounded by life, much of which was not organic or even physical in nature.

Many years later, I wrote the book, *Techno-Elementals*, about the life in the things that we build and that surround us. If you'd like further details, that's the place to look!

The Blessing Partnership I discussed earlier is the simplest of all partnerships with subtle and spiritual forces. It doesn't use alliance space but is an act of sharing love and appreciation with the life in the world around us, both physical and subtle life. It's a reaching out with the Light of our human presence to bless our world and to say "thank you" for all that it offers us.

Beyond this simple act of blessing, it's also possible to create an alliance space with the techno-elementals in one's environment in service to Gaia. Since I began using the example of my living room illustrating what a Gaian partnership with my local subtle environment can look like, let me continue in that vein with my local techno-elementals.

As I described earlier, my living room contains two sofas, a couple of chairs, a television set, a coffee table, three end tables, and so on. There's a rug on the floor. My coffee cup sits on one of the end tables next to the chair in which I sit as I write these words.

My living room is a subtle ecosystem made up of a variety of objects, each of which is a techno-elemental; that is, each of them is a unified field of living, sentient subtle energy defined by intent, shape, and function as a physical object. Like any ecosystem, the energies of these various techno-elementals connect and interact, which allows me to see them both as an individual object and as part of a larger whole, which in this instance is the energy field of the living room. Thus, the white upholstered sofa in front of the living room window is its own thing, and it is also part of the "landscape," the "ecosystem," or interior character and furnishing of the living room as a whole.

I could attempt to form an alliance space with each object in the living room, but as there are dozens of objects (pictures, carvings, candles, plants, lamps, decorations, and so forth) in addition to the furniture and the rug, that would be time-consuming. Given the interconnected nature of the subtle ecosystem represented here, it is also not necessary. If I form a partnership with one object, I can expand that energy to embrace the whole subtle ecosystem of the living room and thus all the objects, all the techno-elementals, in the room. In effect, an alliance with one can become an alliance with all.

As before, our objective here is to connect the living energy of the techno-elementals within our environment—whether that environment is our home, our work area, or someplace else where we are—with the Light and the new energies moving through Gaia from the cosmic dimensions. It creates the opportunity for the techno-elementals to absorb however much they can of these new energies, helping to "ground" them and make them part of the physical world. Every little bit counts!

A key question to answer when creating alliance space is what the function or intention of the prospective partner is. With what am I coming into resonance? In the case of a techno-elemental, one answer could be, "To be a good (whatever-it-is)." Thus, the intent or function of the techno-elemental of my sofa is to be a good sofa.

But this is a simplistic view and a human-oriented one as well. The techno-elemental life within the sofa doesn't necessarily know that it's a sofa or even what a sofa is (though it can recognize, I've discovered, that its role is to provide a place to sit or lie and, if possible, to provide an energy of comfort). What it knows is that it is a field of evolving subtle life and part of a larger ecology of subtle life. I should also say here that I have encountered techno-elementals, particularly in artistic objects or things crafted and not simply manufactured, that know quite clearly what they are and what their use is…and part of that identity is to engage with and give expression to human creativity, making them a blend of human and elemental energies.

Attuning to Techno-Elemental Partners

As an exercise example, for my techno-elemental partner and point of contact with the community of techno-elemental life within my living room, I'm choosing the chair in which I am sitting. I love this chair! It's comfortable, it fits my body and vice versa, and I can happily sit in it with my iPad on my lap and write.

- As before in creating alliance space, I affirm my sacred identity. I affirm my ability through the practice of the Path to connect with my own Stellar Core, my own soul Gift, and thus with its connection to the realms of Light. I am not just David sitting in this chair. I am an incarnational Presence in touch with the wholeness of the world, a Gaian Human affirming his role in that wholeness.

- From this inner place of attunement, I reach out with love from my sacredness to the sacredness of the chair, not simply as a chair but as a vessel of subtle and spiritual life, different from my own but still a part of God. I come into resonance and appreciation with the function of the chair as a chair, providing me a comfortable place to sit and work, but more deeply, with its function as a field of evolving life. This is life in the simplest stages of incarnation, engaging in its way with the energies of matter and of physical reality and learning from that engagement.

- A techno-elemental, whatever its form or structure—and this can be infinite in nature—is still at heart a unit of divine life experiencing beingness and existence in the physical universe and in the three Zones beyond. Though my chair and I are of vastly different capacities and states of consciousness, in essence, we are the same thing: the sacred in incarnation within the wholeness of creation.

- It is this kinship, this sense of fellow-life, with which I resonate and to which I reach out in creating alliance space. We are allies in the unfoldment of life within the world.

- Once I feel this deep connection, transcending chair

and person, then I attune as fully as I can to the new spiritual energies, the unfolding Light, within Gaia. I see the techno-elemental life and I as sharing this experience, both of us in our own ways open to and receiving this new Light. I see the field of this new Light vibrating outward to all the community of techno-elementals within my living room, bringing us together into a shared space of communion and attunement to what is unfolding within Gaia.

- As with the subtle environment, I close this exercise by giving thanks to all the techno-elementals within my living room and specifically to the life within my chair. I release it from the alliance space, closing that particular link (though not the love) between us. And as before, I always end such a session by reaffirming my own Sovereignty, Presence, Self-Light, and Gift.

Before we go further, it's important to emphasize that these different circles or layers in the "Path of Contact" are not separated from each other by hard boundaries. We are dealing with a planetary ecology here, the metabolism of a living being, Gaia. Permeability of boundaries and communion of consciousness are often the order of the day, a natural feature of the subtle environment. This means, for instance, that the subtle environment and the techno-elementals that are the subtle organisms living within that environment are interconnected. What affects one can affect the other. This is true as we go "up the chain," so to speak, to higher, more complex forms of spiritual life, though the effects will differ as the vibrational difference increases.

At the same time, each type of subtle organism, each "layer" of subtle life in the "Path of Contact" receives, digests, assimilates, and shares Light in its own unique way. It's not enough to say, "I'll help the techno-elementals align with and assimilate the new energies," (though if this is all we do, it's still a significant service). The Intelligence within the subtle environment will align and assimilate differently, adding its own unique value.

Nature Spirits and the Subtle Commons

Let me describe, as best I can, what the subtle environment of the natural world around my house is like. I live on a street with other houses, a stereotypical American suburb; a mature housing development that started in the middle sixties. The neighborhood is filled with a mix of evergreen and deciduous trees, common in this part of the Pacific Northwest of the United States. As I've mentioned, we are in a valley surrounded by "mountains" that are actually the foothills of the Cascade Mountain Range immediately to the east of us. A seven-mile-long lake, Lake Sammamish, dominates the valley, fed by rivers coming down from the mountains. There are several dormant volcanoes nearby, Mt. Rainier to the south of us being the most well-known. To the west of us is Lake Washington, then Seattle, Puget Sound, and the Olympic Peninsula beyond, with the Olympic Mountain Range. Beyond that is the Pacific Ocean.

The consequence is that the overall subtle environment of this area contains all four elemental energies of earth, fire (the volcanoes), air, and water. I can attune to this from within my house, but if I'm sitting on my front lawn, I can become very aware of the richness and diversity of the subtle energies flowing and moving in the subtle atmosphere around me.

For instance, I can feel spiritual energies emanating from the nearby mountains, especially from Mt. Olympus in the Olympic Mountain Range many miles to the west, a mountain to which I am, for reasons I don't fully understand, particularly attuned.

I can feel energies and blessings coming from the Deva associated with Lake Sammamish, a feminine presence I think of as the "Lady of the Lake."

I feel energies coming from the rocks and soil of the earth itself, as well as from the surrounding foothills that tower over us to the east and south.

I feel energies coming from the trees, especially the tall fir trees.

There are energies I feel whose sources I cannot identify, energies that feel benign but whose purpose is mysterious to me.

In other words, there's a lot going on! But my awareness, I'm sure, is nothing compared to the sensitivity and awareness of the various subtle organisms—the nature spirits—living and operating in the subtle environment around me. I can only guess, based on my limited experiences, what their world is like.

I mention all this in order to explain just what a "nature spirit" is, at least in my understanding. If the subtle environment is akin to the interstitial fluid that surrounds and bathes our cells, then the nature spirits are intelligent "transfer and exchange" mechanisms that allow nutrients to pass from that fluid into the etheric and physical structures that are the "cells," i.e., the plants, animals, rocks, soil, water, and so forth.

As I write this, I'm looking out the windows in my living room. To the right of my vision are two tall Douglas fir trees that separate our property from that of our neighbor. Directly in front of me, on the other side of the lawn, is a young dogwood tree. Beyond that is the street, on the other side of which are more neighbor's houses. Focusing on the dogwood tree, I'm aware of its innate spirit, its sacred life. But

I'm also aware of spark-like beings who move about the tree. I call them sparks because they resemble points of light, little fireflies flitting about the leaves, but in fact, they could take on any form they wish, including that of a human being. For that matter, I may not be seeing the nature spirits themselves at all, given that they are subtle beings, but the effects of their work as energies move between them and the tree.

Each of these beings is an intelligent and powerful entity, a spirit of nature, whose task is to ensure that the dogwood tree, in this instance, is able to access and assimilate those subtle energies within the subtle environment that will be most useful to it. Meanwhile, nearby there are other nature spirits that are doing the same thing for the Douglas fir. The subtle environment is the same for both, but each is selecting those qualities from that environment that will best service a particular physical species.

In other words, the nature spirit is a being who has access to the wide range of subtle energies available in a particular environment and can discriminate and select those qualities and energies that will nourish the particular physical life to which it is attuned.

A nature spirit is more than just a conduit, though, a being through whom energies flow from one point to another. They also draw different subtle energies into themselves and recombine or reconstitute them to meet the unique conditions and needs of the physical lives they are seeking to help. That is, they can produce from within themselves a particular subtle "etheric chemical" that's needed in the moment by drawing on elements from the environment around them. They create as well as transmit.

This is not a simple task. It is one, I think, that a master human chemist or biologist would find daunting.

There can be a tendency to think of nature spirits as

simple beings, but they are far from simple. They are highly intelligent and highly skilled. They are the indispensable workers in the networks of energy and Light that make up both the ecology and metabolism of Gaia.

And they are highly collaborative.

It was the Fall of 2018. I was writing at my desk when I became aware of an unexpected subtle presence in the room. Turning, I saw a small human figure standing nearby, perhaps five feet or so in height, dressed in an outfit resembling a tunic over trousers. He had on a small, pointed hat.

His overall vibe definitely was different from any of my usual subtle colleagues, none of whom appeared to me in such a definite way in any event. Nor did he feel like a nature spirit. Frankly, I had no idea who or what he was. My friend and Lorian colleague, Jeremy Berg, had been visited from time to time by Kobolds, a type of Faerie being who lived in a house he owned, but his description of them (in fact, he painted a picture of one of them) was different from the being that stood before me. Unknown though he might be, he was smiling and giving off a friendly vibration, and he was obviously waiting for me to acknowledge him. So, I said "Hi!"

As soon as I opened the door, so to speak, I felt myself in touch with a most amazing consciousness, one that simultaneously felt youthful and full of vitality and very ancient, as ancient as the earth on which my house was sitting. I was also immediately aware that this being had immense power not at all represented by his size or the simplicity of his appearance, a power balanced and filled with love.

What followed was an experience I still have difficulty putting into words. Let me preface this by saying for many years when I would tune into a nature being, it was always on a one-to-one basis. That is, I would connect with the nature spirit associated with the maple tree in my backyard or with the Deva of a fir tree or the life within a rose bush. I would be aware of other such beings active in the subtle environment, but always as individuals—or perhaps as a cloud akin to a cluster of fireflies. What I was missing in these experiences was a sense of the interactive, interdependent ecosystem of which these individual beings were a part.

First, I became aware that this being—whom I whimsically called "Bob"—was a kind of Gaian being I had not yet encountered; indeed, to this day, I still don't know if he was entirely of the Devic and nature kingdom or whether he was also part of the Faerie world (something I'll talk about later). What I do know is that he was a steward or caretaker of the subtle ecological wholeness of a particular area, which happened to encompass the land on which my house stood and probably much of the surrounding neighborhood as well.

There is a process my subtle colleagues use in which a subtle or spiritual being gathers my consciousness into his or hers (or its!), allowing me to "piggyback" on their awareness, seeing and experiencing what they see and experience. This is what "Bob" did. I found my point of view moving out of my own body and into his, at which point he showed me the subtle environment of my backyard in a way I had never experienced before.

I was aware of all the different subtle nature beings that were active in this subtle environment but now I was aware of the energy connections and flows of living forces and qualities moving between them. In particular, what struck me was the love that each subtle nature being, no matter how specific or different its function or characteristics might be, had for all the others. This went beyond anything like affection but was a sense that no single being could do what it was doing unless all the others were doing what they were doing. Each different type of nature being had its own unique task to fulfill, and it drew on its own sources of energy for doing so, but it also drew upon all the others, just as they drew upon it.

Searching for words to describe this, it was as if each being was a valuable and needed resource for the other subtle beings. They were "shared resources" for each other. So, in addition to whatever energy a particular being was bringing to its work and to whatever natural phenomenon it was serving, there was this love, appreciation, and caring being shared, just as members of a team can love and care for each other.

There are different metaphorical images that I could use to describe this. The relationship of members of a choir, to each other, to the choir as a whole, and to the music they sing comes to mind. The synergy and love of a deeply bonded team with each other is another possible example. But the image I chose was that of the "Commons."

Living in an old New England village as a young teenager, I became familiar with the idea of the Commons. This is a piece of land that is shared in common by all the families and individuals of the village. It cannot be owned by a person but is there to benefit all—and everyone takes responsibility for its care and well-being. Historically, such Commons were often shared grazing land for sheep or cattle or could be the site of a community garden. The point is that it was a resource that everyone shared, and everyone cared for.

This was the feeling I got from my experience of the subtle ecosystem of my backyard that day; that every being was a resource that benefited every other being and was in turn loved and cared for by every other being. There was a sense that each being was able to do what it did because everyone else was doing what they did, and all were supported by all. Everyone was a resource of sacredness and energy for everyone else.

I call this phenomenon, the "Subtle Commons."

The Subtle Commons is much more than a shared energy field. It's the embodiment of a shared ecological and metabolic connectedness. It's made up of appreciation, mutual caring, support, and love.

Following the Path of Contact, we have worked with the subtle environment and with the techno-elementals that are part of our human-built environment. The next step is to expand beyond the human into the natural world. The nature spirits that are part of our neighborhoods may be the easiest with which to take that step.\

From where I live, I can be in a wilderness forest within ten or fifteen minutes. Hiking through a dense Pacific Northwest forest is a beautiful experience, but the encounter with the subtle forces in that forest is very different from what I meet in my yard or neighborhood. I suppose it would be the difference between meeting the family dog and a wolf in the wild.

I don't mean by this that one is dangerous, and one is not, only that the nature spirits in my neighborhood are used to human energies. They are not "domesticated" but they are familiar with human beings and the kind of emanations we generate. They may even incorporate such energies into the work they do in nourishing their plants. In the wild forest, though, I have encountered nature beings who have little if any experience with humans and thus may not know how to blend with the subtle field I have to offer. It is not beyond question that if their environment has been damaged or destroyed by human interference and action, such as clear-cutting a forest, they may even feel hostile or angry towards members of our species.

For this reason, unless you are skilled or familiar with working with subtle energies and would not be discomfited by a "wild" encounter, I recommend that for this next step on the Path of Contact, you work with nature spirits that inhabit the areas around where you live or work and who have been regularly exposed to—and are familiar with—human energies and consciousness.

To continue using examples from around my own home in tracing the Path of Contact, I'm going to create an alliance space with the nature spirit or spirits who work with a large maple tree in our backyard. Here's an example:

Attuning to Nature Spirit Partners

- As always, I begin by affirming my sacred identity. I affirm my ability to connect with my own Stellar Core, my own soul Gift, and thus with my connection to the realms of Light.

- From this inner place of attunement, I focus on the love that I have for the maple tree itself and its spirit. Why? Because this is a common ground that I can share with a nature spirit associated with this tree. It is also motivated by love for the tree which it serves. Its intent and its function are to help the tree with its life and its growth. If I share this intent, then I and the nature spirit come into resonance. Connection is possible.

- From my sacredness, then, to the sacredness of the maple tree nature spirit, and from my desire and intent through love to bless the maple tree, to the equivalent desire and intent within the nature spirit, a foundation is created for alliance space.

- Once I feel this deep connection between the maple tree nature spirit and myself, then I acknowledge and give thanks and love to it for all its service. I take a moment just to appreciate this being and all that she does, and to communicate that appreciation. I bring my love and spiritual energy into resonance with it so that I can add my strength and blessings to it as it does its work with the maple tree. I want this nature spirit to know she has a human ally, that she is not alone. Together, as allies, we bless the maple tree.

• Then I attune as fully as I can to the new spiritual energies, the unfolding Light, within Gaia. I see the nature spirit and me as sharing this experience, both of us in our own ways open to and receiving this new Light. I see the field of this new Light vibrating outward through the subtle commons to all the community of nature spirits in my backyard—and beyond—bringing us together into a shared space of communion and attunement to what is unfolding within Gaia. I see this new Light flowing into the maple tree and into all the plants associated with all the nature spirits sharing this attunement in this moment through the subtle commons.

• I close in this example by giving thanks to the maple tree nature spirit for its partnership. I release it from the alliance space, closing that particular link (though not the love) between us. And as before, I always end such a session by reaffirming my own Sovereignty, Presence, Self-Light, and Gift.

Devas and Angels

As we move to the next level in our Path of Contact, we find ourselves reaching out to those beings known as angels and Devas. Here we are at the threshold of the two higher Zones, the threshold between the subtle and spiritual worlds. Angels and Devas are perfectly capable of operating within the subtle worlds and the subtle environment—and do so—but their native habitat, so to speak, is in the spiritual realms.

Many people, I've found, use the terms "Deva" and "angel" interchangeably. Are they the same thing? My understanding is no, though I readily admit that there are times when I cannot tell the difference between them—and times when it makes no difference. But on the whole, they have different functions and deal with distinct, though often interrelated, aspects of Gaia's metabolism and ecology. For this reason, I deal with them as separate phenomena.

Devas

The word "Deva" means "Shining One" in Sanskrit, a term that could be applied to any number of different subtle and spiritual beings, but which has come to be used primarily with respect to the intelligent spirits that overlight and oversee the development of nature in all its parts. I've heard Devas called the "architects" of nature, and I think this is a useful and accurate analogy.

In my experience, Devas work with the relationship of spirit to form and matter, giving shape and substance to spiritual ideas and then overseeing the development and maturation of those forms. For example, the maple tree in my backyard is part of a species of tree called "maple" with certain distinct characteristics. At some point in the evolutionary past, a spiritual idea was conceived of such a species by one or more Devas. This "idea" (for want of a better term) is not the same as Plato's primal essential form. It is the seed point for development, a point of beginning, the same as if I said, "I have an idea to write a science fiction novel." The final work may end up very different from my initial idea—it would evolve in the writing of it—and yet still fulfill my wish to write a science fiction novel.

The point, though, is that a particular Deva takes responsibility for nourishing the idea of "maple tree" into physical reality, overlighting all the maple trees in the world, including the one in my backyard.

In her work with the Findhorn Foundation Garden in northern Scotland, Dorothy Maclean contacted the Devas of every variety of plant they put into the garden and received from that intelligence precise instructions on how to enable that plant to thrive in the Scottish environment.

It was during my time as a co-director of the Findhorn community that I began to have experience contacting and working with Devas, something that had not been part of my inner education up until then. But Findhorn was not my first encounter with the idea of the Devas as the creative Intelligences behind nature and its phenomena. Living in Redwood City (with a sign boasting "Climate Best by Government Test") on the San Francisco Bay peninsula, I had a close friend who also happened to be my attorney, Leonard Worthington. He and his wife had a house with a large garden in the foothills overlooking Redwood City. I was admiring the beauty and variety of his garden when he said, "It's because of the Devas." I hadn't heard that term before, so I asked him what he meant. "I think of them as the angels of nature," he said. "When I work in the garden, I attune to them and ask their guidance and blessing." The evidence in the garden was overwhelmingly positive, as it was for me years later while at Findhorn.

Devas come in all sizes and complexities and exist at all levels of life within Gaia's ecology. They are essential to Gaia's metabolism and are often the sources of the currents of nourishing and vitalizing energies that flow through the subtle environment. There are Devas associated with particular plants, such as those Dorothy Maclean worked with in the Findhorn Garden. There are also Devas associated with landscapes, such as the Deva of a mountain or of a particular ecosystem or watershed.

For instance, in the valley where I live, I'm aware of energies flowing from at least four different Devic sources. There is the majestic and powerful Deva overlighting Mt. Rainier to the south of us whose influence covers the entire Puget Sound region. As I've written above, I'm also particularly attuned to the energies flowing from the Deva of Mt. Olympus in the Olympic Mountain range to the west. Though these are both mountain Devas, the influence I feel from each is different as the energy from Mt. Olympus feels personal in ways the energy from Mt. Rainier does not. There are also Devas of the surrounding foothills and a Deva whose influence overlights the valley as a whole like an umbrella of Light. Then there is the energy arising from the Deva of Lake Sammamish, my "Lady of the Lake."

These are the main influences I feel, and like different voices in a choir, each sounds a different note or chord in the music of life and energy that nourishes all of us living here in this valley, human and non-human, physical and non-physical. In addition, there are different Devas of the different variety of trees that fill this valley and my neighborhood, my maple tree being one of them.

It goes without saying, I hope, that in the subtle commons, all these Devas work and blend together in mutual support, each offering its unique contribution to the Gaian whole and all co-creating synergy and the emergence of a unified field of blessing.

To demonstrate alliance space with a Deva, I am choosing as my example the Deva of Lake Sammamish. I could pick the Deva of my maple tree, or of the Douglas Fir tree in my front yard, or the Deva of the rose bush my daughter has planted in our garden. I have an abundance of choices. But my "Lady of the Lake" stands out as she is a powerful and unique feature of our valley.

Lake Sammamish is a five-minute walk from our house. Our housing development boasts a small park with a playground and, as part of it, a small beach. When our children were small, my wife and I would bring them down to this beach to play in the water. It was during one such excursion that I became aware of a presence within the lake itself and saw a feminine figure rising partway out of the water, a semi-human form made entirely of Light and water. At first, I thought this was a water spirit of some kind, but tuning in to its energy, I realized it was the Deva of the lake showing herself to me.

This lake is surrounded by homes, many of them quite large with their own marinas and boats. There is also a large State Park at the south end of the lake with a large beach. There are often swimmers in the lake and boats as well.

My point is that the Deva of this lake is well acquainted with human beings who use its water recreationally and holds them within her love as well as the non-human denizens of the area. She generates her own sacred energies, but at the same time, she seems to act as a receptor for energies coming from the surrounding mountains, some as far away as Mt. Rainier, some fifty or sixty miles to the south. I have felt her taking the energies from the mountain Devas into herself and reconfiguring them to be of greater benefit to the ecosystem immediately around her and within her influence. In effect, she assimilates, digests, and re-broadcasts spiritual energies that come to her and which otherwise might be of too high a frequency to be used by the life in the valley.

There are more powerful water Devas in the area. Lake Washington is the largest nearby lake, and then, of course, there is Puget Sound itself, whose Deva I have seen once while crossing the Sound on a ferry; a towering, majestic, and totally awesome being that seemed inhuman to me in the scale of its power. By comparison, the Lady of my lake is cozy and accessible, a "good neighbor" Deva with whom I can feel at home. That's why I chose her for my example of this Deva practice.

Attuning to Devic Partners

- I begin by affirming my sacred identity. I affirm my ability to connect with my own Stellar Core, my own Soul Gift, my Presence, and thus with my connection to the realms of Light.

- From this inner place of attunement, I focus on the love that I have for Lake Sammamish, the valley that surrounds it, the nearby mountains, and the city of Issaquah itself at the south end of the valley. Why? Because this is a common ground that I share with my Lady of the Lake. It is also motivated by love for this valley, and all its inhabitants, human and otherwise. Its intent and its function is to be of service to the subtle, spiritual and physical life of the valley. If I share this intent, then I and the Deva come into resonance. Connection is possible.

- From my sacredness, then, to the sacredness of the Deva of Lake Sammamish, and from my desire and intent through love, to bless the Issaquah valley to the equivalent desire and intent within the nature spirit, a foundation is created for alliance space.

- Once I feel this deep connection between the Deva and myself, then I acknowledge and give thanks and love to the Lady of the Lake for all her service. I take a moment just to appreciate her and all that she does and to communicate that appreciation. I bring my love and spiritual energy into resonance with her so that I can add my strength and blessings to her as she does her work. I want her to know she has a human ally, that she is not alone. Together, as allies, we bless the valley.

- Then, I attune as fully as I can to the new spiritual energies, the unfolding Light, within Gaia. I see the Deva and I sharing this experience, both of us in our own ways open to and receiving this new Light. I see this new Light flowing into the valley, awakening all within it to the new possibilities which this Light brings. I ask that my partnership with the Deva bring the new Gaia that much closer into being.

- I close this practice by giving thanks to the Deva of Lake Sammamish for its partnership. I release it from the alliance space, closing that particular link (though not the love) between us. And as before, I always end such a session by reaffirming my own Sovereignty, Presence, Self-Light, and Gift.

Angels

I have had more experience over the years with Angels than I have had with Devas. One reason is simple. Most of my work has been with people rather than with nature, and most of the angels I've encountered have been those who work with humanity in one way or another.

As I understand the function of an angel, it is one of ministering to the development of soul and consciousness, and the nourishing of sacredness within a particular form. If a Deva is like an architect, designing the structure of the house, the angel is concerned with what happens within that house to make it a home. At least the angels whom I have encountered have been concerned with the course of human evolution, i.e., what happens within us of a spiritual nature.

As discussed earlier, each of us has a guardian angel as one of our natural allies or Entelechy. It serves as a kind of executive officer for the soul in doing what it can to further our incarnation's spiritual and subtle evolution and development.

Many angels I encounter are associated with organizations and the buildings or places they occupy. The basic principle seems to be wherever human beings are working together, one or more angels are overlighting the collective field of energy these humans generate seeking opportunities to further the love, the sacredness, the wholeness, and spiritual well-being and development of the humans within that field. How successful they are can depend on the humans, of course!

For instance, our local grocery store has an angel overlighting it. When I go shopping there, I'm aware of its presence, and I always acknowledge it with love and appreciation when I cross the threshold into the store itself. There's a good energy in the store, and people genuinely seem to enjoy working there as well as shopping there.

Many years ago, when my children were little, one of my daughters lobbied that I take her to McDonald's for a Happy Meal. I think a certain toy she wanted was being promoted with the Happy Meal, never mind the food itself! I resisted as I was not overly fond of fast-food places. But she persisted, so I gave in.

We were standing in line when suddenly to my inner vision, the McDonald's roof disappeared, and I found myself looking up at a blue sky with three towering angelic figures surrounding a much smaller, younger-looking being. They identified themselves as angels overlighting the McDonald's corporation, not just the particular restaurant we were in. "We are about to enter the world stage," they said, indicating the younger looking angel, "and take on a new engagement with humanity." Then, the vision ended, leaving me, I admit, shocked. McDonald's was the last place I had been expecting to run into angels of such power. Talk about a Happy Meal!

A week later, there was an announcement on the news saying that McDonald's was opening a restaurant in Moscow, a first for the Soviet Union. It was considered a breakthrough in "food diplomacy," introducing Muscovites and ordinary Russians to something that as Americans, we took for granted - hamburgers and fries. When I saw this, I knew that this was the "new engagement" that the angels had mentioned. The younger angel was representative of this new connection, the outcome of which was not assured but which was hopeful of expanding into something good in connecting two populations together who were otherwise suspicious of each other.

This brings up an interesting question: How are angels "born" and how do they develop?

As I understand it, angels emerge out of the stellar realms, in response to a need or a creative endeavor which requires or would benefit from their presence and service. The angel itself is "full-blown," so to speak, but its connection to the world is not and may need to develop. This is what I saw with the "adult" and "child" angels in my McDonald's vision. The angel of McDonald's in the Soviet Union did not have a fully developed vehicle of connection to start with.

Let me use my experiences at Findhorn as an example. When I lived at Findhorn in the early seventies and was first tuning into the Findhorn Angel, it was—at least to my vision—a simple presence. Essentially, it was the equivalent of a zygote in the development of a human being, the beginning of what I think of as a "subtle and spiritual organism." This was by no means its "true" or complete nature and only represented as much of itself as could connect and interact with the community at that time.

As the community grew and became more diversified and complex, the form that the Angel took—its connection to the evolving Findhorn experiment—was able to grow and become more complex, too. After I left Findhorn in 1973, my family and I would visit the community from time to time. Each time we did, I was aware of how the Findhorn Angel was growing in its ability to express itself.

This was especially true as an international Findhorn-connected community developed. Over the years, thousands of people have visited this eco-spiritual center in Scotland, attending its classes, spending time as part of the community, and so on. When these people left, many of them continued to stay in contact with each other and with Findhorn itself. This created a network of connected energy around the globe which in turn provided an expanded field of contact and expression for the Findhorn Angel and its energies. This enabled the angel to grow from a local angel operating in one small area in Scotland to being a planetary angel, one that has multiple points of contact and connection with humanity and the earth, rather than, say, one or two.

The angel of my home, by contrast, has my house and our family as its primary point of contact, and that is all it needs to perform its function. A "planetary" angel, on the other hand, either has or requires points of contact with a diverse group of human beings representing different races, ethnic groups, nationalities, etc., who are located in equally diverse places around the globe. The Findhorn angel grew to become such an angel.

Interestingly, in recent years, especially after COVID shut

everything down for a year, the Findhorn Foundation, which had been the primary organizational "body" for the Findhorn experiment, ceased to exist. In its place, however, new organizations, businesses, and groups, all resonating with the Findhorn energy and purposes, have been emerging. It's as if from being a single-celled organism, with the Foundation as that cell, the Findhorn Angel is now multi-cellular, its energy and presence manifesting through a diverse collection of interrelated and collaborative human endeavors. It allows the Angel to express a more complex version of itself. Of course, this puts a challenge before everyone involved to find ways of working together as a whole eco-spiritual endeavor within which their individual contributions are honored and able to thrive while still giving expression to a larger wholeness. But then, coordination is always an issue for multi-celled organisms!

The morphology of angels is complex; compared to them, we as incarnate humans are more like single-celled creatures while they are multi-cellular. This has nothing to do with our shape or physiology, of course, but everything to do with our consciousness and the ways we can become fixated in a particular direction or around a particular belief and thus unable to see the world in more holistic, systemic ways. We do, though, have it in us to become "angel-like" in our perspectives and actions. This is what the emergence of the Gaian Human is all about, and what the new Gaian energies seek to promote.

In giving an example of creating alliance space with an angel, I have many options. I could do so with the angel of an organization I would like to assist, or one for whom I am working. I could do so with my own guardian angel or the guardian angel of another person whom I would like to bless. But keeping with the "down-home" theme of my examples,

I'm choosing to form alliance space with the being that I call the House Angel. This is the angel that overlights our house as a structure, our property, and the home that is created within these things. Most homes have a House Angel—or as some might call it, the Family Angel. Here's a practice to explore:

Attuning to Angelic Partners

- I affirm my sacred identity and my ability to connect with my own Stellar Core, my own soul Gift, my Presence, and thus with my connection to the realms of Light.

- From this inner place of attunement, I focus on the love that I have for my house as a structure, for the home, and for all who live within it. This is common ground that I share with my House Angel. Its intent and its function are to be of service to the subtle, spiritual and physical life of this house, the property around it, and the people within it, both inhabitants and visitors. If I share this intent, then I and the angel come into resonance. Connection is possible.

- From my sacredness to the sacredness of our House Angel; from my desire and intent through love to bless our home to the equivalent desire and intent within the angel; a foundation is created for alliance space.

- Once I feel this deep connection between the angel and myself, I acknowledge and give thanks and love to it for all its service. I take a moment just to appreciate this being and all that it does, and to communicate that appreciation. I bring my love and spiritual energy into resonance with the angel so that I can add my strength and blessings to the work it does. I want the House Angel to know it has a human ally, that it is not alone. Together, as allies, we bless this house and its home.

- Then, I attune as fully as I can to the new spiritual energies, the unfolding Light within Gaia. I see the angel and me as sharing this experience, both of us in our own ways open to receiving this new Light. I see this new Light flowing into the house, filling its energies with the new possibilities that this Light brings. I ask that my partnership with the House Angel bring the new Gaia that much closer into being.

- I close this practice by giving thanks to the angel of our home for its partnership. I release it from the alliance space, closing that particular link (though not the love) between us. And as before, I always end such a session by reaffirming my own Sovereignty, Presence, Self-Light, and Gift.

The Commonwealth of Light

At this point in our journey along the Path of Contact, we are wholly into the "highest" or most complex and intense of the three energy Zones, that of the spiritual realms. At this point, our contact is almost always soul to soul, though many of the beings we might encounter here are capable of engaging with us in a less-intense, more accommodating Zone such as the subtle realms or even the subtle environment.

I should reiterate that when I use terms like "higher," "more complex," or "more intense," I'm speaking from the point of view of my everyday consciousness and subtle energy field. When I say "more complex," I don't necessarily mean more complicated. Many spiritual principles and energies are very simple, such as love. What I mean is that they engage my being—my mind, my emotions, my body, my subtle field, and so on—in more holistic ways, demanding more points of contact.

Let's take love, for instance. The principle of loving is as simple as it gets but think of all the many ways you can love, and the different forms love takes. For me to love my wife or my children is easy and comes naturally. But what about loving a stranger? What about loving someone who is outside the range of what I think of as "normal?" What about loving an enemy? Or loving more than one person at a time? What about loving a group? A place? A nation? Humanity as a whole?

Christ expressed love, and no one was outside the field of his love, even those who sought to kill him. How simple and how complex is that? If you bring me a gift or food or water when I'm thirsty, I can love you. Will I love you if you come with a spear, with nails and a cross? How fully, how completely, how deeply will I embrace you, forgive you, treasure you, uplift you in my heart, hold you blameless before God as you drive the spear into my side or the nails into my hands?

This is what I mean by "complex." Love is able to touch and embrace and bless a person no matter how different he or she is from ourselves, how kind, or how threatening.

Now think of joy, of courage, of hope, of laughter, of humor, of many other qualities, and realize that each of them has depths that go beyond the simple definition of an emotion or a response to life. Each of them can be more complex than we imagine.

This is the nature of the spiritual realms. This Zone extends us, expands us, opens us in ways we may never have experienced before, ways that at first seem uncomfortable, perhaps fearful, or even impossible, but only if we approach it and view it from the more limited perspectives of our physical consciousness. For our soul, this Zone is not complex or difficult, higher, or more intense.

It is home.

This is why any practice that connects us with our soul and allows us to become familiar with our soul's way of being is important. It makes the extraordinary ordinary.

This is why I feel something like the Path I've been describing and a concept like the Gift are important for they help us see ourselves in new and expanded, vital and joyful, holistic and empowering ways. They give us something we can practice, bringing the felt sense of our sacredness deeply into our bodies, our minds, and our hearts. I keep repeating that it's not the only way. Each of us is unique, so each of us needs a way that speaks to us in our uniqueness in the moment. But if you find it helpful, then please avail yourself of it. Think of it as a gift from me to you!

With this as a preamble, let's look at the next step on the Path of Contact. I call this the "Commonwealth of Light."

Rather than talking or writing about "Zone One" (or "Three," depending on where you're counting from, up or down), or about the "Spiritual Realms," I like to call this the Commonwealth of Light. This is because to my inner vision and current state of development, at this level distinctions tend to disappear or blur. Rather than seeing distinct nature spirits, Devas, or angels, I see and experience collectives of Light and consciousness. It's not that individuality ceases to exist. It doesn't. But it becomes shared and "participatory" in ways challenging for an incarnate mind so used to distinct boundaries to comprehend. Am I in touch with one angel or with a hundred? One Deva or many? One soul or a cluster of souls? And does it matter? I am in touch with Light manifested through a synergy of presences, one and many, many and one.

It is in this Commonwealth of Light that I encounter what I think of as truly planetary and cosmic beings, "Shining Ones" whose fields of life and focus encompass the globe as a whole, or the relationships between Gaia and all the transplanetary life that make up the solar system. Here, for instance, I might encounter a Solar Angel or even a Stellar Being.

In such encounters, the Solar Angel or the Stellar Deva, or whatever or whoever it is, may shape a tiny part of itself into something familiar my mind can recognize and process. It might take on the form of a human being, for instance. But I try to engage with such beings soul to soul, that is, from a level of my own consciousness and being for whom multi-dimensionality is familiar and ordinary. That is when, at least to some extent, I'm able to see such a being as it really is, though seeing and comprehending are not necessarily the same thing.

When I attune to the Commonwealth of Light, I have often received the following message:

If you could see the world as we see it, we would be better able to work with you.

This has to do with resonance. The greater the resonance between two beings, the deeper and more effective the partnership or collaboration can be between them. This is true for us in the physical world. It's even more true for beings in the subtle and spiritual dimensions. Put in human terms, if you and I share the same perspective on the world, we can work more closely and easily together than if our perspectives are different or even in opposition. If I say the world is a good place and you say it is a fallen, evil place, then at some point our ways of understanding and engaging the world are going to diverge.

This also has to do with love. In the spiritual worlds and with the Commonwealth of Light, love is an essential mode of being and doing. These beings bring love to the world. But this is not true for us. We *can* love the world, but for many of us, the world is not a lovable place. It is a place of challenge, of difficulty, of suffering, even of darkness. We look out at the world and see conflict and violence; we see injustice and oppression; we see damage and destruction. We see a world that is imperfect and broken, particularly in its human aspects. The angels and Devas can see this, too; they are not blind to human dysfunctions and suffering. But this is not the nature of the world they see. The world they see is one of Light.

Is the perspective of the Commonwealth of Light more real than the one that we have? Do they have a truer grasp on the nature of things than we do? A mystic would likely say yes. But in my experience, the spiritual realms are not denying the reality of the world as we see it; at least, they are not denying that it is real to us and therefore the world with which we are dealing. As I said, they are not oblivious to human suffering or the challenges that face us. But—and this is a subtle point—they *are* saying that they could work more closely and in greater resonance with us if we *also* saw the world as they do. They are inviting us to participate in a shared awareness of the world as a manifestation of Light. By sharing in this perception, a resonance is created between us that strengthens the bonds through which they can partner and work with us.

They are inviting us to be part of the Commonwealth of Light within the physical world.

When I am in touch with angelic, Devic, or spiritual modes of consciousness, I am aware of the sacredness, the beauty, the wonder of the world, and I am filled with love for the earth and all within it. As a result, my life becomes a clearer conduit for their blessing. Put simply, a spiritual being can partner more closely with someone who loves and rejoices in the world as they do, seeing it as a manifestation of the sacred.

One does not have to have psychic or subtle perceptions to see the world with eyes of love. Partnership with spirit is not limited to a select few. Also, one doesn't have to deny or ignore the suffering and broken aspects of our world. These things call out to our compassion and our efforts towards wholeness and healing, just as they do for the angels, Devas, and all the souls that make up the Commonwealth of Light. But it is a powerful act of resonance with the spiritual worlds to open our hearts and minds and choose to hold love for the world and to see the beauty of life within it. From such a choice, blessings can flow, and the presence of Light made closer than before.

For the most part, I do not attempt alliance space with Presences in the Commonwealth of Light. There is no need. There either is contact or there is not, and if there is, it is soul-to-soul, sacredness to sacredness, immediate, intimate, and profound. Partnership is not an option in the Commonwealth of Light; it is the nature of what is. If we are in connection, in communion, we are automatically in partnership.

But there are exceptions; when a Commonwealth Presence operates in the subtle realms where possessing and expressing a specific form is important. For example, the Angel of a nation, such as the Angel of America, or even the Angel of Humanity as a collective field. A personal example of this for me, which I've referred to earlier, is the Being who overlights Mt. Olympus in the Olympic Mountain Range west of Seattle.

Ever since I moved to Issaquah and the Puget Sound area in 1984, I've felt an affinity with this mountain. I don't know why in particular. It's not as if I've hiked its slopes or even visited the Olympic Mountain Range very often. But the affinity is there. And it's an affinity not only with this mountain but with what I've come to think of as a "Council of Mountain Devas" that represents the Commonwealth of Light.

My story of this affinity begins with a ferry trip to Orcas Island. This is one of the islands in the San Juan Island chain that lies in Puget Sound between Seattle and Vancouver, Canada. Orcas Island is home to Indralaya, a beautiful retreat and educational center founded by members of the Theosophical Society in 1927. It was one of the places where I gave workshops and classes on occasion.

Rising over the center of Orcas Island is Mt. Constitution, the highest point in the San Juan Islands. A hike up the mountain rewards you with a magnificent view of Puget Sound and its many islands. It also, on one particular day when I made that hike, opened me to a contact with the local mountain Deva who in turn introduced me to a collective field of consciousness shared by mountain Devas around the world.

I called this field of shared consciousness the "Council of Mountain Devas." What was clear from the beginning was what I was perceiving as this group of shining beings was, in fact, a projection out of a much deeper, more complex state of planetary beingness of the Commonwealth of Light. They were, in fact, more than just the Devas of particular mountains but worked in collaboration with those Devas to deliver a stabilizing energy into the whole planetary field. It was as if all the great mountain chains and ranges in the world—the Himalayas, the Rockies, the Andes, the Pyrenees, the Alps, and so forth—were acting collectively as a planetary "spine," providing a flexible inner structure that was holding the world together during this time of profound change and new beginnings.

Mt. Olympus and the Deva of that mountain became for me a point of contact with this "Council" and with the

Commonwealth of Light beyond it.

In practicing the Path of Contact, I can use this mountain and its overlighting Deva as my touch point and partner with whom to create an alliance space.

Here again, is a Path of Contact practice for your consideration:

The Path of Contact Practice

- As with all the earlier exercises, I begin by affirming my sacred identity and my ability to connect with my own Stellar Core, my own soul Gift, my Presence, and thus with my connection to the realms of Light.

- From this attunement, I focus on the love that I have for all mountains and for Mt. Olympus in particular. Then, I broaden that love to take in all of the world, celebrating the beauty of the Earth and all life upon it. This love for the planet as a whole is the common ground that I share with this mountain Deva and with the Commonwealth of Life of which it is a part. Its intent and its function are to be of service to the subtle, spiritual and physical life of the world. If I share this intent, then I, the mountain Deva, and the Commonwealth of Light come into resonance. Connection is possible. A foundation is created for alliance space.

- Once I feel this deep connection between the mountain Deva, the greater Light of the Commonwealth of Light, and myself, then I take a moment just to appreciate this Deva and the Commonwealth of Light it represents, and all that they do. I bring my love and spiritual energy into resonance with them so that I can add my strength and blessings to the work they do, so that I, too, may be an expression in the world of the Commonwealth of Light.

- Then, I attune as fully as I can to the new spiritual energies, the unfolding Light within Gaia. I see the mountain Deva, the Commonwealth of Light as a whole, and as I share this experience, all of us in our own ways open to and receive this new Light. I see this new Light flowing into the world, filling the earth and all upon and within it with the new possibilities which this Light brings. I ask that I may be a partner with the Commonwealth of Light to bring the new Gaia that much further into being.

- I close this practice by giving thanks to the Deva of the mountain for its partnership. I release it from the alliance space, closing that particular link (though not the love) between us. And as before, I always end such a session by reaffirming my own Sovereignty, Presence, Self-Light, and Gift.

Faerie

I debated whether to include the Faerie race and kingdom in this book. This isn't because they're not important; they are. They are a vital part of Gaia's planetary ecology. It's because I have very little experience with them, at least that I know of. It's possible that the being I wrote about who introduced me to the subtle commons, the being I whimsically called "Bob," is a Faerie being, but I don't know that for sure…and he has never said one way or another. Other than him, though, I can only think of one other encounter that might be said to be Faerie in origin, though again, I'm not sure.

We have a crow family that lives in the trees in our backyard. For many years, we have fed them, and they have become less and less afraid of us (if they ever were!). They are far from being pets, but we have a comfortable and amiable relationship. My wife and I can sit on the back porch and have a crow or two come and sit nearby, just relaxing and sunning itself, seeming to enjoy our silent companionship. (My wife taught the crows not to caw loudly when on our porch or in the backyard, and for years now, they have honored that agreement.)

One night, I had a vivid, lucid dream experience. I felt that someone was in our kitchen. I got out of bed, walked down the hallway from our bedroom, and stepped into the kitchen which has a sliding door that opens onto the back porch. There I discovered two people, a man and a woman, standing at the stove, dressed entirely in black, each with long, flowing black hair. The man was explaining to the woman what the stove was, and I caught the words, "It's something humans do." At this point, they became aware of my presence standing in the doorway and turned around and looked at me. I had the distinct impression that these were two of our crows, temporarily in human form, the one explaining to the other something about our human world. There was nothing frightening about them, nor were they frightened to see me. There was a friendly acknowledgment of my presence, and then they disappeared, and I woke up.

Native Americans speak of the "animal people" who preceded humanity in living upon the earth. These beings are part of the Faerie race, elders upon the planet in every sense of the word. I felt that I had been privileged to encounter two of the crow people, perhaps two who in their bird form lived in our trees and visited us on our porch. If so, it is the only encounter with Faerie that I can point to.

Which is why I can't write about them. I don't have the experience base from which to do so. Others, like my friends and colleagues John Matthews, R. J. Stewart, and Orion Foxwood, do have many rich experiences working with the

Faerie world and have written extensively and eloquently about them. I recommend investigating their books if you are interested.

What I do know is this: my subtle colleagues often call the Faerie race, "the Children of Gaia." Where we as human beings largely originated as Cosmic Humanity from the stellar realms, perhaps coming from distant star systems (as spirits, not in spaceships!), the Faerie race originated here, on earth, from Gaia's own stellar nature and planetary Gift as a separate line of evolution from our own and contributing their own unique gifts to the wholeness of the world. They are truly the Elder Race, a Gift of Gaia, being part of the world before Cosmic Humanity entered the picture.

Can one create an alliance space with a Faerie? I think in theory, yes. The principles are the same: intention, resonance, hospitality, love, and connecting sacredness to sacredness around a shared service. In dealing with them, it's important to realize that whatever they look like (and they can certainly take on a human shape; Bob did, if Bob was a Faerie), they are not human and may not share (or even understand) human values, motives, or objectives. The possibilities for miscommunication and misunderstanding are certainly there.

But my understanding is that Faeries have a deep love for Gaia, and if you can share and communicate that, at least, I think partnership could be possible. But I have never done it, so I have no example to share with you. It's an area for future exploration.

The Sidhe

My contact with the Sidhe (pronounced *shee*) came about in an unexpected way. I was sitting in my living room reading when I felt an unfamiliar but strong energy field enveloping me. It was not like any subtle or spiritual being I had contacted in the past. As I turned my inner attention on it, I could sense, as if through a fog, the shape of a woman's face which took on greater definition and clarity as I concentrated. It was a sharp, angular face, not without its beauty but not entirely human, either. There was a sense of wildness about her, something feral, though not dangerous.

I could feel that she was attempting to form a telepathic link with me, but it was hard as her energy was so different from mine or of any of my subtle colleagues. We both persisted, though, and over the course of a few minutes, a clear channel of communication was established.

It was then she told me she was a representative of the Sidhe and that she came with a proposal to create a tool that would facilitate contact between her people and incarnate human beings. This tool turned out to be a card deck. During this first of what became many meetings, she presented me with a complete outline of what this deck would be like and how it could be used.

I subsequently shared this information with my Lorian colleague and the publisher of Lorian Press, Jeremy Berg, who then discovered that he, in turn, was being contacted by this same Sidhe woman. Out of this three-way partnership, the *Card Deck of the Sidhe* was born, along with a couple of books of conversations I had with our Sidhe contact, who identified herself as Mariel.

Unlike the subtle and spiritual allies I've discussed in this book, the Sidhe occupy a unique place. This is because, as I understand it, they are not subtle beings per se but are a species of humanity incarnating in a less-dense vibration of matter that is still part of Gaia.

The Sidhe and Faerie beings are often confused with each other. There are certainly similarities, but the Sidhe are not Faeries. They are not Children of Gaia, nor are they the oldest race to evolve upon the earth. They are our cousins, descendants of Cosmic Humanity who for various reasons chose not to fully incarnate into the denser forms of matter the way we have done. Like us, they are Children of the Stars.

Like us, the Sidhe have access to Gaia's subtle and spiritual dimensions, as well as, when needed, the subtle environment. But while there are spiritual Sidhe with highly developed consciousnesses, the Sidhe are not spiritual entities in the same way that angels and Devas are. The Sidhe have a range of individual development just as human beings do.

But there are significant differences between us. Our experience with dense physical matter gives us capacities the Sidhe lack, just as someone who works in construction and carries heavy blocks of stone and concrete every day is going to develop a different set of physical muscles than someone who spends their day sitting, reading and teaching classes. On the other hand, the Sidhe have an attunement to Gaia and its wholeness that we have forgotten. This puts us in the position of being able to complement each other.

I have never created an alliance space with a Sidhe; I've never needed to. Their mode of contact with me is unique and different from any other non-incarnate, non-physical being, relying on what feels like a soul-infused, heart-mediated telepathy. This, plus the fact that they are not subtle beings, made me pause and debate whether they should be included in this book of partnering with spirit.

I don't have an example to use for contacting the Sidhe. They have always made the first step in establishing contact with me, and then I have followed up on the relationship—and the resonance—that we established. However, the *Card Deck of the Sidhe* is a tool that Mariel gave us explicitly for developing lines of contact and communication. The card deck and manual are readily available from Lorian Press or

Amazon, and I would recommend it as a place to start if this is an avenue you would like to explore.

Would such an exploration be worthwhile? I would say yes. The Sidhe are involved in the emergence of the Gaian Human and are themselves conduits for the new spiritual energies entering the overall ecology and metabolism of the Earth.

Earlier in this book, I discussed the development of two Sheaths around the Stellar Core of our Cosmic Humanity; a Gaian Sheath and a Humanity Sheath. The Sidhe shared in this development, but there is a third Sheath that humanity took on as a condition of incarnation which I did not mention at the time. This is the Sheath of Physical Matter.

The picture I presented earlier should look like this to be fully complete:

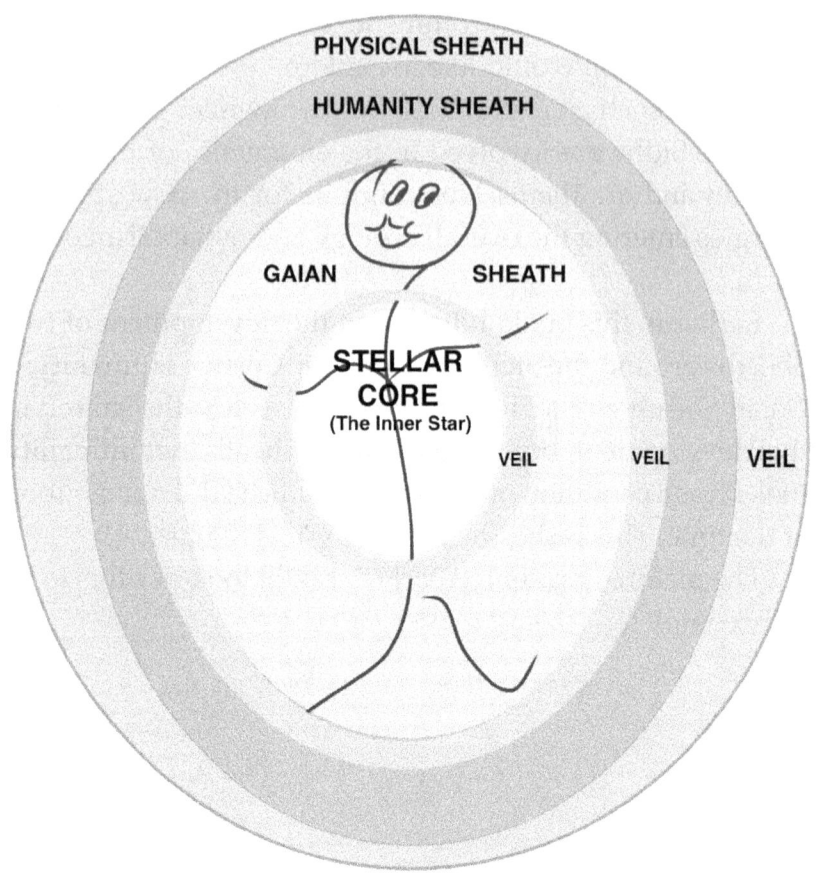

As I said earlier, for humanity to fully incarnate, veils had to be created to temporarily cut off the influence of the Stellar Core and the Gaian Sheath so that an independent human consciousness could develop. But the Physical Sheath acted as a veil in its own way, which in many cases exacerbated or exaggerated the effects of the other veils in isolating our consciousnesses from Gaia's living presence.

The Sidhe are those human souls that never took on the Physical Sheath or the Sheath of Dense Matter. Did they experience the other veils as well as part of their evolution? I don't know. Neither Mariel nor any other Sidhe with whom

I've been in contact has said. My guess is that they did, but not to the same degree and not with the same "gunky" consequences as happened with incarnate or non-Sidhe humans.

The result is that the Sidhe are and have largely always been in touch with both our shared human Stellar Core and with the life and wholeness of Gaia manifested through the connections and sensitivity provided by the Gaian Sheath.

So, are the Sidhe the same as the Gaian Human?

No.

But they are close.

The full Gaian Human isn't simply a person who has made whatever inner veils are there transparent, healed, or has cleared away whatever "gunk" had collected in and around those veils and has brought their Stellar Core, their Gaian Sheath, and their Humanity Sheath into resonance and harmony. He or she is also a person who, through love and understanding, is transforming their Physical Sheath—i.e., their relationship with the physical world—so that it, too, vibrates, reflects and shines with the joy and Light of the Stellar World. In effect, he or she is a person who is able to "ground" the new energies into the world of matter, transforming the outer world from a "veil" into an expression of Gaia as a stellar planet, a "star of life."

A Gaian Human would look like this:

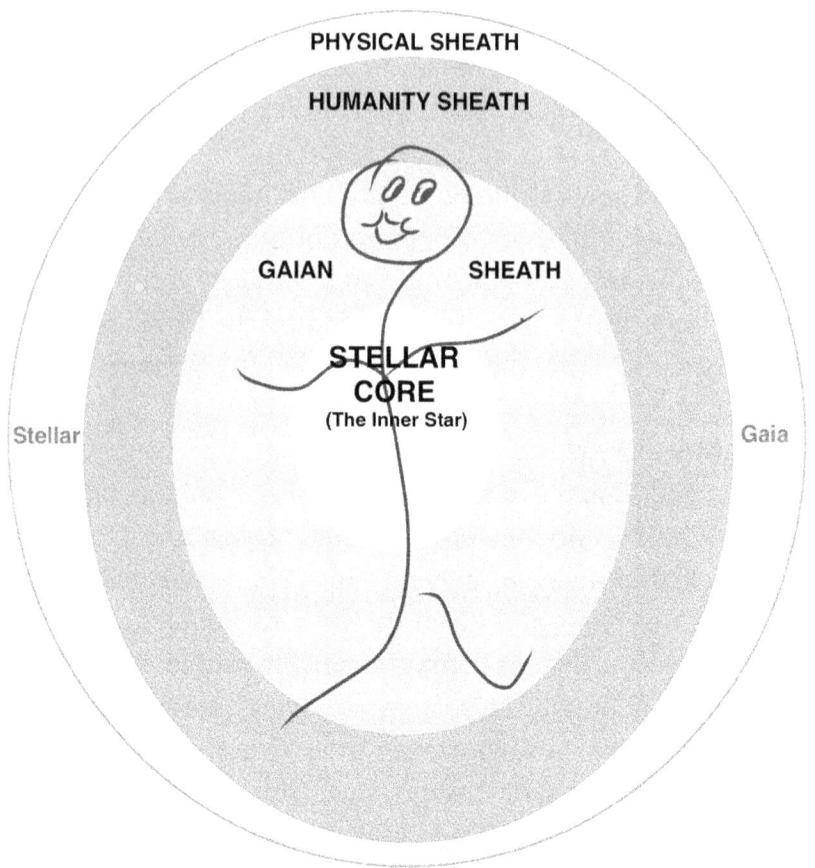

The Sidhe do not have the experience with dense physical matter to be able to do this. On the other hand, the Sidhe do bring with them the vibrations of resonance and harmony between the Stellar Core and the Gaian and Humanity Sheaths. They can assist through their energy and partnership with the dissolving of the "gunk" within the human veils and also with the dissolving or rendering transparent the veils themselves.

In other words, they can give a definite boost to the emergence of the Gaian Human within us. Next is a visual equation:

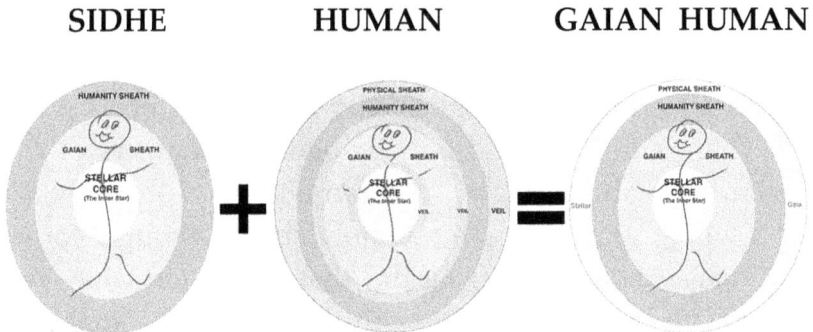

In this process, the Sidhe may also learn and benefit from the experiences of incarnate human beings, opening them to new possibilities and capacities, with the ultimate destination being the reunification of the two sides of humanity in the Light of a new Gaia and a new Gaian Human. It may take hundreds of years for this to happen, but right now, we are taking the first steps.

Gaia

We come now to the ultimate Gaian partner: Gaia itself.

In effect, when we partner with any part of Gaia—with the subtle environment, with a techno-elemental, with a nature spirit and the subtle commons, with a Deva or an angel, with the Commonwealth of Light, or with Faerie or the Sidhe—we are partnering with Gaia.

As I recounted in *Part I: The Foundations*, one member of our Entelechy, our group of natural incarnational allies and partners, the "Incarnational Elemental," is itself a representative of Gaia as a kind of "human nature spirit." It is, as they say, "closer than hands and feet" and always available for contact.

I have never attempted to form an alliance space with Gaia because, for me, Gaia is not a being, at least not in the same way an angel or a Deva or a nature spirit is. It is the life, the presence in which I am embedded as part of the world. Everything I do can create partnership with Gaia, or as is so much the case with human activity today, disrupt it.

There *are* Devic and angelic beings, members of the Commonwealth of Light, who can and do represent Gaia as a whole, and there are humanly created thought-forms of Gaia, such as "Mother Earth," that can do the same. You can create an alliance space with them using the approach I have described. But they are not—and cannot be—Gaia in its wholeness.

The challenge with personifying Gaia and giving it a specific form is that we can then forget that Gaia is everywhere and everything around us. Gaia is also us. We are already in a deep and profound, eons-long partnership that began with Cosmic Humanity and led to our becoming part of the life of the world.

We are already allies.
This is what we have forgotten.
This is what we must remember.

The Path of Light

Throughout this book, I've been discussing Paths and offered one such path based on my experiences with the subtle and spiritual worlds. But there are many paths into Light and many paths for bringing Light into the world. What is important is establishing a practice that offers a consistency of connection and flow, something that builds over time, develops coherency, and thus increases its capacity to deliver.

One of my subtle colleagues, reflecting on what I'd been writing, said, "This process you are describing could become very powerful if it were repeated, using the same partners and thus deepening a groove along which Light can flow." The pattern he suggested is much the same as the way learning takes place in the brain as networks of neurons are repeatedly connected in sequence until that pattern becomes part of the "wiring."

With that in mind, I make the following suggestion for creating a "Path of Light," a particular "groove" of attunement along which Light and new energies repeatedly flow and become established as part of the "brain" and thinking of Gaia. Next is a picture to illustrate this:

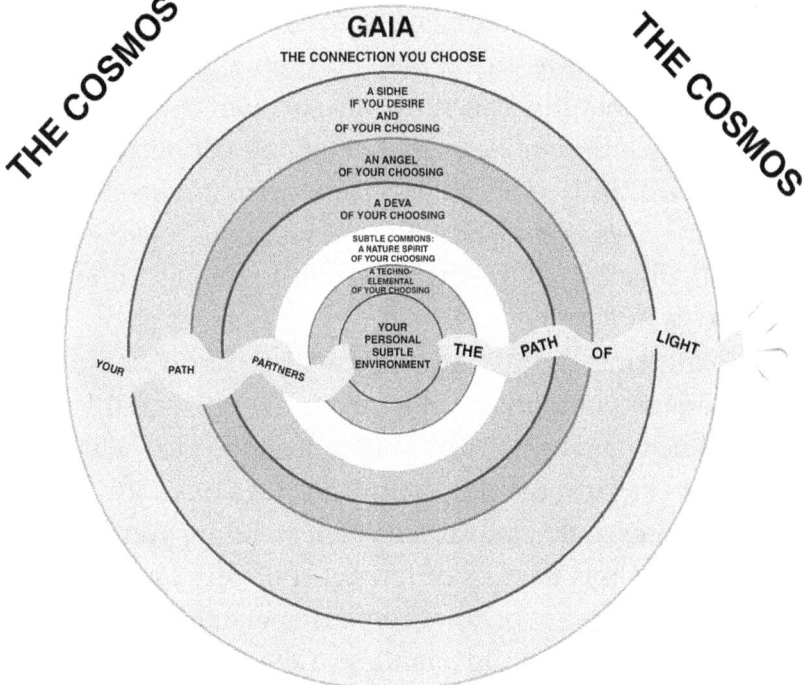

Consider the following adaptation of a picture I used earlier to describe the Path of Contact. Here you are creating a "Path of Light" by using the same "Path Partners" in a regular way. For instance, using my earlier examples, my Path of Light would begin with the subtle environment in my living room, expand to alliance space with my chair as a techno-elemental, then with a maple tree nature spirit, the Deva of Lake Sammamish, the Angel of my house, and as part of the Commonwealth of Light, the Angel or Deva of Mt. Olympus in the Olympic Mountain Range to the west of me. I could even include a contact with Mariel as a Sidhe connection.

In effect, I am starting with a small alliance space and then expanding it as I go, and at each level with each "Path Partner," I am invoking and attuning to the new Light, the new energies within Gaia.

The key is not spending too much time with each partner but seeing them all as part of a chain, a network of Light, along which new energies can flow, all partners in manifesting a new Gaia. It's your experience of the connection—and the flow within it—that relates to heaven and earth that is important. This is the Path of Light we share together—the "Grand Alliance," if you wish—and it is what unites and empowers us.

Do this once a day, and you will see how the power and connection builds, both for your own personal Path of development and contact, and as a contribution to Gaia within the subtle environments around you. As one Path builds and resonates and achieves a level of stability, you can then create a new one, using a different set of Path Partners. The important thing is not to become dispersed but to ensure that the Paths you build manifest a consistent and steady flow of Light.

There is another very important thing to keep in mind. All the examples I've shared of alliance space are only suggestions based on my own experience. They are not recipes you have to follow.

Like any relationship, the depth and power of the

experience depends on the participants involved and what they bring to the table. Each person, each subtle or spiritual being, is unique. For this reason, you need to be sensitive to the situation and aware of what you bring as your Gift, as your Presence...in addition to what your prospective partner may bring by way of their intent, function, and love. In this process, you are not a follower of someone else's way. You are an explorer and a creator of your own way, tailored to the partnership and the service you wish.

Presence, Not Information

There is another important distinction I want to make about the approach I've been describing. The object of Partnering with Spirit here is not to gain information, though it's possible information may be gained. The object of partnering with spirit is to establish a presence of Light, both within yourself and within the world. You are not seeking something solely for yourself; you are performing a service.

This is not how people have usually approached the subtle and spiritual worlds throughout history. The emphasis has been on receiving information in the form of guidance, prophecy, teaching, and revelations. There is nothing inherently amiss with this. Why shouldn't we turn to other levels and types of consciousness for a new, different, or wider perspective than we might have otherwise? Why not seek out guidance from a wiser source?

The challenge is one of discernment. How do we know the information we receive from a subtle or spiritual source is accurate? How do we know if it's helpful? Not all subtle or spiritual beings are necessarily wiser or more knowledgeable than us, and even when they are, they may not have the experience or background to fully understand human nature or the conditions we face while in physical incarnation. As a consequence, their information or advice might be faulty.

For example, in working with my subtle colleagues, I quickly learned that most of them had no sense of time as it passed for me. They might say that something was going to happen "soon," meaning that the energy pattern of a future event was close to the etheric and physical plane, but "soon" could turn into days, weeks, even months in my time.

Furthermore, unfortunately, there is the possibility of running into a subtle being whose motives are to make trouble, or to deliberately mislead or simply to gain the energy of adulation and worship by pretending to be a "master" in the inner realms.

The issue of discernment is an important one when dealing with subtle and spiritual beings, but it's beyond the scope of this book. Fortunately, it's less of an issue when the focus is on being a presence of Light and service rather than on getting information.

Soul on the Ground

The challenge for humanity is that we are incarnate in physical bodies, with the veils that incarnation brings with it or can create, and we are dealing with the trauma from our past.

The strength and importance of humanity is that we are incarnate in physical bodies and are a part of the earth as well as a part of heaven. We are souls on the ground which is where we need to be to deal with the trauma from our past and be able to erase the veils.

And, where we need to be to form a Gaian Alliance in bringing the new face, the new energies, and the new life of Gaia into form and expression.

Let me repeat the thesis of this book.

Gaia, the World Soul, our "Star of Life," is going through

what amounts to an initiation: the taking on of new spiritual energies with a resulting need to assimilate and integrate new intensities and possibilities of Light and sacredness. This is causing changes across the board throughout the spiritual, subtle, and physical ecology and metabolism of Gaia.

As part of this process of assimilation and integration, there is a need to "ground" these new energies to make this cosmic Light a part of the physical earth. Throughout the world, there are species and beings who are working to do this, but this is also humanity's special responsibility. We are the souls on the ground, the ones who possess both the Stellar Core and the Gifts of Light from our cosmic beginnings and who are part of Gaia, and part of the earth.

In this, we are like a tree, our leaves soaking up the sunlight and our roots bringing nourishment deep into the earth.

We are a conduit between heaven and earth, all three "Zones" of consciousness and life coming together within us.

We also possess the gift of an imaginative, creative intelligence, able to introduce novelty and emergence into the world, to dream not only of what has been or what is, but of what could be…and then to bring those dreams into reality.

At the moment, we are creating less of a dream and more of a nightmare on the earth, but this is because we have forgotten who and what we are. We have forgotten our ancient partnership with the living planet. We have forgotten the Gifts our souls bring "to the ground," to the earth, to physical, incarnate life. We have forgotten how to honor, appreciate, and love our incarnations and to see them as an expression of a sacred identity.

We have forgotten how to be whole people in a whole world.

But we can remember.

The time to remember is now.
It is time for the veils to fall away.
The Light is calling to us.
Gaia calls to us.
And from our deepest selves, we call to us.
It is time for partnership.
It is time for the Gaian Alliance.

The Gaian Alliance

We formed a Gaian Alliance when we first came to this world as Cosmic Humanity and joined in partnership to help Gaia fulfill its dreams, its intents, and its destiny as a star of life.

As Gaia enters a new phase of its life, it is time for us to forge this Alliance again. It is time to touch our star heart and to bring our Light and sacredness back into conscious partnership with our living world.

My own work over the years, especially with the development and practice of Incarnational Spirituality, has been to understand and respond to the call of our time. It's a call to us as individuals to recognize the Light within us, and it's a call to Humanity.

How we each hear and answer this call is up to us. I have long felt and taught that the first step is to acknowledge our sacredness and to live our lives in the Light of its Presence within us. We are not born on this earth in a physical body by accident whatever the outer circumstances may have been. We are here by our soul's choice as a soul Gift to the world.

But we are also here as part of a larger enterprise, the life of Gaia and the well-being of the world. We are here as expressions of an ancient alliance, one that seeks renewal and rebirth in the world at large.

We have the power to reforge this Gaian Alliance. Its

reality lies within us, just waiting for us to externalize it through our actions, our relationships, and our partnerships.

The good news is that we don't have to do so alone. Others who recognize this call and respond to it can join with us. Partners - human, subtle, and spiritual - are available. It's an *Alliance*, not a solo journey or endeavor. But it's up to us to do the work that collaborative partnerships based on love demand.

I do not promise that any of this will be easy. I cannot. We all know or can sense the challenges that a veiled and disrupted world can throw up to block the Light. But help is there. Partners are there. And the new Light of Gaia is everywhere.

May we all know its blessing and its power as we reach out to partner with Spirit in the emergence of a new world.

READING REFERENCES

Should you wish to explore more deeply the topics touched on in this book, here is a recommended reading list.
The following is a list of books I have written that are relevant to the material in this book
Journey Into Fire
Apprenticed to Spirit
The Subtle Worlds: An Explorer's Field Notes
Working with Subtle Energies
Techno-Elementals
Partnering with Earth
The Card Deck of the Sidhe
Conversations with the Sidhe
Engaging with the Sidhe

The following are books by other authors that touch on topics discussed in this book
The Findhorn Garden, by the Findhorn Community
Animate Earth: Science, Intuition, and Gaia, by Stephan Harding
The Wonder-Full World of the Home, by Timothy Hass
The Wonder-Full World of the Home: Second Story, by Timothy Hass
The Call of the Sidhe, by Soren Hauge
The Wild Alliance, by Soren Hauge
The Magic of Findhorn, by Paul Hawkin
To Hear the Angels Sing: An Odyssey of Co-Creation with the Devic Kingdoms, by Dorothy Maclean
The Sidhe, by John Matthews
Meditation as Contemplative Inquiry: When Knowing Becomes Love, by Arthur Zajonc

PARTNERING WITH SPIRIT CARD DECK

The language of the subtle worlds is often not that of words or intellectual concepts such as we are familiar with in our everyday physical lives. Instead, subtle beings often speak through the use of qualities that can inspire intuitive insights.

The *Partnering with Spirit Card Deck*, designed by Jeremy Berg, Deva Berg, and David Spangler, is based on this perspective and is designed to be a companion to this book. The card deck is particularly focused on connection and communication with our natural Allies, our Entelechy.

For further information or to purchase this card deck and instruction manual, please go to the bookstore at www.lorian.org.

www.ingramcontent.com/pod-product-compliance
Lightning Source LLC
Chambersburg PA
CBHW071155160426
43196CB00011B/2091